ARTHUR PENN

series edited and designed by Ian Cameron

ARTHUR PENN

ROBIN WOOD

PRAEGER

BOOKS THAT MATTER

*Published in the United States of America in
1970 by Frederick A. Praeger, Inc., Publishers
111 Fourth Avenue, New York, N.Y. 10003*

© 1969 by Movie Magazine Limited

*Library of Congress Catalog Card Number:
76–91697*

Produced by November Books Limited

Printed in England

'*Arthur Penn is one of the greatest directors in
the world.*"—*Ingmar Bergman.*

Photographs of Little Big Man *by the author.*

*Stills by courtesy of Columbia, Warner-Pathe,
United Artists.*

CONTENTS

44001

INTRODUCTION

'*A living man is blind and drinks his drop.*
What matter if the ditches are impure?'
—*W. B. Yeats,*
A Dialogue of Self and Soul.

What immediately strikes one in the films of Arthur Penn may appear at first glance a superficial feature, but it leads right to the essence of his art: an intense awareness of, and emphasis on, physical expression. Physical sensation (often, but not necessarily, violent) is perhaps more consistently vivid in his films than in those of any other director. Again and again he finds an action—often in itself an unusual, hence striking, action—likely to communicate a physical 'feel' to the spectator, and devotes all his resources—direction of the actors, camera position and movement, editing—to making that 'feel' as immediate as possible, arousing a vividly empathic response. Here, as illustration, are five examples, one from each of Penn's films:
1. *The Left-Handed Gun:* As the McSweens' home is burned, Mrs McSween, distraught, struggles helplessly to check the chaos around her. The sackers unwind reels of printed fabric which brushes and almost entangles her. She collapses, despairing, on the steps of the shed, clutching handfuls of the contents of an overturned barrel (which, overturning, nearly hits her), holding them to her forehead, rubbing them in her hair.
2. *The Miracle Worker:* Annie Sullivan introduces herself to the blind and deaf Helen Keller by thudding down her trunk on the step on which Helen is sitting. The child senses the vibration, feels with her hand. Penn cuts to a close-up of the hands as Helen's feels Annie's, the delicacy of contact suggesting that the fingers are the child's ears and eyes. Helen raises Annie's fingers to her nose and smells them.
3. *Mickey One:* During the credit sequence, a girl sprawled across the bonnet of the car Mickey is driving, presses her lips to the windscreen. The camera is positioned inside, so that we see the flattening of her lips, the misting of the glass by her breath. Mickey turns on the windscreen wiper, which rises up to touch the girl's open mouth.

4. *The Chase:* At the height of the climactic riot, Mary Fuller, drunk and hysterical, suddenly stuffs part of the pearl necklace she is wearing into her mouth and bites. The necklace bursts. Some of the pearls stay in her mouth, others scatter on the ground amid car tyres, etc.

5. *Bonnie and Clyde:* C. W. Moss's 'Daddy', infuriated by the sight of his son's tattooed chest, suddenly flicks hot thick soup (or pease pudding) across it from a saucepan with a large spoon. C.W. is in the right foreground of the screen, so that the soup is flicked towards the spectator.

Obviously all these examples carry overtones and implications that go far beyond the immediate physical sensation: in *The Left-Handed Gun*, the emotional associations of the stored goods, the basis of the family's stability; in *The Miracle Worker*, the reaching out to a contact beyond the physical; in

Still: The Miracle Worker—*the first meeting of Helen and Annie.*

Mickey One, the strong phallic-erotic overtones; in *The Chase*, the sense of extreme
emotional pressures. But in all five, the invo-
cation of the spectator's sense of touch is
remarkably potent.

I have selected a few striking moments;
this physicality pervades all of Penn's work.
In no other director's films (possibly excepting
the Westerns of Anthony Mann) does pain
consistently seem so real. The death agonies
of Buck Barrow are but the extremest instance
of a continuous characteristic: think of the
wounding and subsequent deaths of Billy's
friends Tom and Charlie in *The Left-Handed
Gun*, or of the beating up of Calder in *The
Chase*. Everything is done, through make-up,
through the acting, through the whole presentation, to encourage the spectator to empath-
ise as intensely as possible: when Bubber
Reeves is shot at the end of *The Chase*, one
feels the bullets going in. Obviously, any able
director uses more of his actors' resources
than their facial expressions; but Penn seems
to draw exceptionally on his actors' bodies,
to build up characters from characteristic
movements, gestures, ways of walking. Think
of almost any Penn character and you will get
an immediate mental image of the way he
walks, bears himself, uses his hands: Tom in
The Left-Handed Gun, Edwin Stewart in
The Chase, C. W. Moss in *Bonnie and Clyde*.
It is a very superficial view indeed that sees
The Miracle Worker—in which one of the
leading characters can neither see, speak nor
hear, hence can be communicated with *only*
through touch—as thematically marginal to
Penn's work: it stands apart only in its emin-

Still: Bonnie and Clyde.

8

Still: The Miracle Worker.

ently 'respectable' true-life subject-matter, of the kind that wins Oscars for directors ready to give it the conventional 'respectful' treatment. Although Helen Keller isn't really the emotional centre of Penn's film, the first mental image anyone is likely to conjure up of it is of the way Patty Duke *moves*.

Such a mental image is basic to Penn's work: it is, one could almost say, his starting-point. It epitomises, in vividly physical terms, the idea of a soul imprisoned in a physical existence that is inadequate to express it or fulfil its needs. Early in *The Miracle Worker*, Helen's parents argue heatedly about her, while Helen, neither seeing nor hearing, stands between, feeling their moving mouths with her fingers and frantically moving her own, instinctively aware that some form of communication is taking place from which she is excluded. Suddenly, she raises her arm and slaps her mother viciously across the face. Frustrated energies and urges clamouring for an outlet, and often finding it in the messy inadequacies of physical violence: Bonnie Parker, beating on the cross-bar of her bed, then dashing frantically down the stairs, hastily buttoning a dress over her naked body, movements clumsy, vigorous and desperate, to team up with a young man she has seen try to steal her mother's car. The opening of *Bonnie and Clyde* brings the spectator as close as a movie camera can to a direct physical apprehension of reality (each camera position is intensely characteristic), and suggests within a couple of minutes the inner drives that the body part-expresses, part-frustrates.

The characteristic movement in Penn can be described as a groping outwards from that starting-point of the young Helen Keller, an incipient and demanding consciousness locked in the narrowest and cruellest of prisons, towards expression, contact, communication. From one point of view (it is not the whole story), the character at the opposite end of the spectrum is Calder in *The Chase*. If one cannot finally accept Calder as fully embodying the positive values implicit in Penn's films, it is because too much of what so evidently fascinates and obsesses Penn is left aside. But Calder, alone among Penn's protagonists, has a developed awareness that enables him not merely to participate in, but to stand back and *judge*, the life in which most of Penn's characters are more or less helplessly embroiled. *The Chase* implies throughout a tragic and despairing view of the society it portrays—and by extension, I think, of modern civilisation itself. But the tragic sense of the film rises most powerfully to the surface at the moment when Calder, 'the finished man among his enemies', at last succumbs to the all-pervasive violence against which he has so far so uncompromisingly stood out and of which he has been one of the chief victims: when he is driven 'to pitch/Into the frog-spawn of a blind man's ditch, /A blind man battering blind men'—Yeats' lines spring appositely to mind to evoke Penn's view of life untranscended by the awareness of a Calder.

The acute feeling for physical sensation,

Still: The Chase—*Calder escorts Bubber Reeves to the jail.*

then, is balanced by an equally acute awareness of its limitations and attendant frustrations. In a number of cases, physical impediments are given great prominence: Helen is blind, deaf and dumb; Clyde Barrow is impotent; the Salvation Army hostel keeper who tries to bring Mickey One the Word of the Lord is afflicted with a bad stammer. In each case the sense of *physical* frustration is used to suggest the presence of frustrated urges and needs that are more than physical. To these examples one can therefore add others where there is no actual physical handicap but which have in common this sense of frustrated, perhaps scarcely formulated, needs: Billy the Kid's inarticulateness and illiteracy; Mickey One's burden of indefinable guilt; the complex pattern of suppressions and resentments, guilt and hypocrisy in the society of *The Chase;* Bonnie Parker's lack of any values that could provide a *valid* escape from her sense of constriction. Penn in his films to date has given us arguably the most complex and mature treatment of violence in the American cinema. The presentation of violence, the defined attitude to it, differs from film to film (e.g. from *The Chase* to *Bonnie and Clyde*). Yet one assumption remains consistent throughout: that violence in all its forms, from Helen's fury at being forced to hold a spoon, through respectable society's vindictive hunting down of Bubber Reeves, to Bonnie and Clyde's armed robbery, is an inevitable outlet for frustrated urges that can find no other. The escalation of violence into a catastrophic situation beyond anyone's control is a recurring *motif* in Penn, and felt with terrifying intensity: *The Left-Handed Gun*, *The Chase* and *Bonnie and Clyde* are all built on overall movements of this kind, and certain local instances stand out with exceptional vividness: the progression from Billy's first act of vengeance to the burning of the McSweens' home in *The Left-Handed Gun*, the escalation at the climax of *The Chase*. In every case the development into chaos is made possible—indeed, inevitable—by a lack of awareness, a partial or total blindness on the part of some or all of the participants.

If the consciousness of a Calder, then, represents one of Penn's major positive values, it is balanced by another not easily compatible, the response to which is at least equally strong: the feeling for physical sensation leads naturally to an attraction to the instinctive and spontaneous. Penn's most characteristic protagonists—Billy the Kid, Bubber and Anna Reeves, Bonnie and Clyde—possess such qualities to a very marked degree: this is at once what makes them so attractive and what destroys them. Spontaneity is also a prominent feature of Penn's style. The total effect of a sequence like the burning of the McSweens' home is so complex as to be difficult to put into words (and dangerous to attempt: one risks being misleading). There is intense horror, certainly, at the senseless and uncontrolled destruction arising from 'spontaneous' behaviour: Mrs McSween's reactions are central to the effect of the scene. At the same time it is shot with an *élan* that does more than merely express the descent into chaos: there is an inescapable sense of the director's delight, not of course in the destructive behaviour shown, but in the spontaneous flow of expressive visual ideas. The disturbing power of such a sequence lies in one's sense that the communicated excitement of the *creative* act is closely related to the characters' abandonment to *destructive* acts: they have in common the sense of a surrender to impulse. (I am talking here of the effect of the scene on the spectator, and not suggesting that conscious and carefully worked out decisions played no part in Penn's *mise-en-scène*. Clearly, a scene of such virtuoso execution doesn't just 'happen'). Again and again in Penn's films (the supreme example is *Bonnie and Clyde*)

Still: The Left-Handed Gun.

what is felt as most admirable in the characters, their spontaneous-instinctive response to one another (Billy's doggedly reiterated 'I knew *him*', about his late boss, with whom he has exchanged a few sentences), is inextricable from all that is most destructive and disastrous in them. The films very powerfully convey a sense of the tragic impurity of human motivation, of human impulse, of human existence.

'Complexity' and 'ambivalence' are words one can hardly escape from in talking about

Penn. Consider one fully representative sequence: that in *Bonnie and Clyde* in which the Barrow gang capture and humiliate Hamer, the Texas Ranger. Factually, the issue seems simple enough: Hamer is a defender of an unjust and corrupt social order; in his state, Texas, thousands are homeless and destitute. Instead of protecting them, he has left his territory to track down a gang whose outrages are committed against established society and for whose capture there happens to be a large reward. Hamer is not (given the sympathy the film enlists on behalf of the criminals) a sympathetic character. The scene could easily have been played with him as a grotesque butt, in which case its emotional

Still: Bonnie and Clyde, with Sheriff Hamer (Denver Pyle).

effect would have been simple. But instead of making Hamer merely pompous or merely repellent, Penn and his actor invest him with an immense and genuine dignity that produces in the spectator a direct effect quite independent of any question of his motivation. We do not feel, I think, that the man we are shown is activated solely by greed for the bounty. Consequently, we 'feel with' his humiliation as intensely as we 'feel with' the spontaneous fun being had at his expense; we are torn between identifying with Bonnie's delight in her idea of having him photographed with the gang, and with his sense of outrage. What is peculiarly characteristic of Penn is that such complexity of response is achieved without distancing the spectator from the action: we feel on the contrary very closely involved in it. Few directors provoke ambivalent reactions that are so *immediately* disturbing. Two moments in the sequence stand out: Bonnie's kissing of Hamer, and his reaction of spitting in her face; both are given at very close quarters, both provoke this duality of response particularly intensely.

We feel so much affection for Penn's characters: even, often, for the obviously unpleasant ones. There is always something more to them than one could get down on paper in a list of their 'characteristics': an aliveness. Describe the characteristics of Joe Grant, the law enforcement officer in *The Left-Handed Gun*, and one would find oneself with a character on paper almost wholly contemptible. Yet it doesn't quite occur to us to feel contempt for the character on the screen: he is too well understood, he is a human being. It is not a matter of '*tout comprendre, c'est tout pardonner*': we don't pardon his petty vicious-

ness, which we are made to see very clearly and critically for what it is. But we not only see Grant's viciousness and weakness, we see a thinking, feeling, reacting person: we accept our common humanity with him, what he is is contained in us. Most directors are concerned purely with what the character is meant to be in respect to the whole, and it is a perfectly valid way of working, to keep in mind the total pattern and see that each part relates as it is necessary for it to relate. But Penn's people seem often to have an extra

Still: The Chase—*Calder goes to save (and arrest) Bubber Reeves.*

dimension, an aliveness, something that cannot quite be neatly tabulated in terms of their role. Even Hamer, I think, is not entirely detestable. We hate his vindictiveness, his cruel treatment of the deeply hurt, blinded and bandaged Blanche, his life devoted to the single purpose of hunting down and destroying, by any means, two human beings. Anyone else would simply

have shown the vindictiveness, would have treated the character in terms of 'characteristics'. With Penn, Hamer is alive and *feeling:* when he spits in Bonnie's face, we recognise the gesture first as a spontaneous response from a living individual centre, not as an action necessary to the total pattern or even as an 'illustration' of character.

Two important conclusions can be drawn from all this about the nature of Penn's art. One is the openness of his response to experience, expressed in his ability to feel and communicate contradictory reactions to a given situation simultaneously. The emotional complexity of his work is the outer sign of a remarkably complete response to life, of a man alive in body, mind and spirit, able to hold different and even apparently incompatible attitudes in balance. The second conclusion follows from the first: the incompatibility can be resolved only in a tragic sense of existence. In calling Penn's art essentially tragic, I do not just mean that it is full of

Stills: images of incipient or actual violence in The Chase.

violence and pain, sad, or pessimistic. It is rooted in a sense of human nature being in a state of constant conflict between irreconcilable pulls, each of which has its own validity. Tragedy is at a far extreme from nihilism: the sympathy, affection and respect Penn elicits for so many of his characters leaves one with the sense that life is as wonderful as it is appalling.

D. H. Lawrence wrote that as a novelist he considered himself superior to the saint, the scientist, the philosopher or the poet: they each produced 'tremulations on the ether' to which a separate part of man responded; only the novelist's tremulations aroused a corresponding trembling in 'whole man alive'. Just as in the nineteenth century the centre of creative interest shifted from poetry to the novel, so in the post-D. H. Lawrence era it has shifted from the novel to the cinema. The cinema of Arthur Penn is the cinema of 'whole man alive'.

Still: Angie Dickinson in The Chase.

THE LEFT-HANDED GUN

Itself an excellent and self-sufficient film, *The Left-Handed Gun* offers a remarkably complete thematic exposition of Penn's work to date. Returning to it from his later films, one finds certain scenes somewhat laboured and self-conscious (notably, the seduction of Celsa, and the closing sequences after Billy's escape from jail); even here, the use of heavily stylised and leisurely gestures and movements points forward interestingly to Penn's total command of strong and meaningful gesture and movement in his later work. *The Left-Handed Gun* is very clearly the work of the director who was to make *The Miracle Worker* and *The Chase*; what is most striking is its very close relationship to *Bonnie and Clyde*. Indeed, it offers so many parallels that there is a danger of missing certain major differences between the two films.

We would take William Bonney, on his first appearance, for a near-idiot, were it not for the movements of his eyes and body. As he answers questions (all of which have to be repeated) with a monosyllable or a gesture, we become aware, beneath the inarticulateness and apparent obtuseness, of an animal-like intuitive awareness of people. His eyes focus on first one and then another of Tunstall's men as they speak, and his body half turns towards each, as if he were 'feeling' them with some physical sense. This impression is subsequently modified (he is, at the start, in a state of extreme exhaustion), but throughout the film we have the sense of instinctual urges and perceptions reaching only partial conscious definition and never subjected to the test of rationality.

The opening sequences juxtapose and contrast different sorts of 'knowing'. Against Billy's instinctual knowing is set the purely verbal factual knowing of the man who tells Tunstall about Billy's past. He judges Billy solely by what he knows about him, and direct contact fails to modify his judgement in the least. Between the two is Tunstall, one of the most entirely admirable figures in all Penn's work, and killed in the first ten minutes of his first film. In Tunstall the two sorts of knowing—the conscious and the instinctual—are harmonized. The relationship between him and Billy is beautifully realised in two short scenes (both of which were cut by the distributors for the film's British release, perhaps on the grounds that no one is interested in little things like motivation, so let's get on to the shooting). The first suggests the limitations of Billy's way of knowing: nothing exists for him beyond what he has experienced or seen for himself, and it doesn't occur to him to look behind what he observes for motives, causes, purposes. The two men see a gipsy wagon moving across a hillside. From Mexico, Billy says. Yes, agrees Tunstall, they come from all over the world, Mexico, Spain, Hungary . . . No, Billy insists, Mexico. He describes with considerable intensity the Easter ceremony of burning a straw man, clearly visualising it all as he speaks. Why do they do that? Tunstall asks. Billy hesitates (he has never thought to wonder about it), then shrugs expressively: it's no concern of his. The images of the straw man and the gipsies are to be taken up at important points in Billy's later development.

The second scene suggests Billy's gropings towards a wider understanding, under Tunstall's influence. Before these two scenes, we have been given the essential information about Billy's past: his father abandoned wife and child when Billy was still young; at the age of eleven Billy stabbed to death a drunk who insulted his mother. Tunstall is sitting reading; Billy edges up, at once curious about the book and desiring contact. Tunstall shows a complete understanding of Billy—he realises without being told that Billy can't read, he senses the boy's needs. He offers to teach him to read, and also to explain things to him. He shows him a chapter-heading, 'Through a Glass Darkly', explaining it as 'something you see that you can't make out'. Billy thinks, then suggests 'An enemy'. 'Or a friend,' says Tunstall. The scene is crucial to all that follows. Tunstall is clearly becoming the father that Billy never had: a possible opening out of Billy's character and outlook is suggested in the touching sense of reciprocal sympathies, the young man's groping towards a wider apprehension balanced by the old man's evident pleasure in finding a 'son' to guide. The killing of Tunstall the next morning is consequently felt as destroying a possible future for Billy, a progression towards wholeness. But Billy also links Tunstall with his mother (who used to repeat passages from the Bible to him that she knew by heart); Tunstall never carries a gun, he needs Billy's protection as his mother used to need it. Hence Billy's reaction to Tunstall's death is to repeat the pattern laid down in his childhood: revenge is a psychological necessity to him. It is also the only means left him of expressing the strength of his feelings for Tunstall.

Only at the end of the film is Billy beginning to learn, painfully, to look behind the surface appearance of things (himself included) and take into account the complexity and muddle of existence. For him, the main issue is simple: four men, one of them the sheriff, have been responsible for Tunstall's death; there is no hope of appealing to the law, since the law is the corrupt sheriff; therefore, he must kill the four men. On the one hand, he fails to take into account—because he is incapable of examining it—the possible impurity of his own motivation: he mistakes personal psychological need, in which there is a further complication of pride and obstinate presumption, for the simple sense of moral outrage which, though genuinely there, is only part of a complex whole. On the other hand, he fails to take into account the possibility that the four men may not necessarily all be equally guilty: that he is dealing with human beings, not cogs in a machine. He also fails to take into account the possible consequences of violence, both for himself and for others.

The sequences culminating in the burning of the McSweens' house take us right to the heart of Penn's treatment of violence. From the scene of Billy's vigil over the coffin in McSween's house (another scene the British distributors considerately removed in case we found it too taxing: happily, the 16 mm. prints are intact), where he becomes possessed by his sense of mission, Penn cuts to the joyous

Photograph: Arthur Penn (in white) directing Tunstall (Colin Keith-Johnston) and Billy (Paul Newman) in The Left-Handed Gun; *McSween (John Dierkes) looking on.*

release of Billy's mock parade to the victrola music. The exhilaration is infectious: we don't know the cause of it yet. The following scene in the hotel room (Charlie in the bath-tub, Tom in long underwear) reveals that Billy has discovered the names of the four men. We share sufficiently the sense of moral outrage for our sympathies to be partly with the revenge, though there is already a fairly strong counterbalance: the physical details of the scene make the two young men whom Billy is trying to draw in seem very vulnerable —particularly Charlie in the tub, arms in the water up to the elbows so that he appears a limbless trunk. Charlie's decision not to help ('No, sir,' with an awed and decisive head-shake) and Tom's sense of the outrage to justice in the murderers' going free (his repeated 'Ought *not* to'), are given exactly equal weight.

The shooting of Brady and Morton precipitates one of those uncontrollable escalations of violence that Penn handles with such mastery. Revenge provokes revenge; the innocent suffer and die; the 'worthy citizens' avenging the killing of their sheriff abandon themselves to an orgy of brutishly unreflecting destruction that ceases to have even a pretextual connection with justice or morality: we are close to the world of *The Chase*. Billy's earlier '*I'm* the law', at once heroic and presumptuous, gets its echo in Mrs McSween's helpless and desperate 'Where's the law?' as she watches her home burned down with her husband in it. There is a sense of violence constantly present in society, just below the surface, awaiting a pretext to erupt. That the audience partly *wanted* the precipitating act of revenge has its clear relevance here.

There is more positive feeling for the society depicted in *The Left-Handed Gun* than in any of Penn's subsequent films. One has, of course, to take into account here Penn's feeling for time and place, and the differences between the various societies depicted, but it seems to me that one can trace in his work a progressive disenchantment with established society, balanced by a correspondingly intense feeling of people's need for it: another facet of the tragic tension that characterises his work. The society of Madero is not created in much depth: the Mexican characters are comparatively conventional, Pat Garrett's wife, for instance, having little of the presence that even the most minor figures in Penn's films are usually endowed with. There is consequently little sense of implied background life to what we actually see. Nevertheless, the sequences of the party and (more especially) Pat Garrett's wedding sufficiently realise the concept of social stability to make its subversion very disturbing. Social values, in fact, are most powerfully projected through the character of Garrett himself.

The precariousness of social order, the constant presence of potentially subversive and violent forces within it, is subtly suggested throughout the film. One detail of background life in Madero we *are* shown is a cock fight. The celebration that culminates in the burning of a straw figure (to which fireworks are tied) suggests a delight in violence and destructiveness irrespective of its religious significance. Saval, the gentle and tolerant man who protects and shelters Billy, is a gunsmith. His

Still: Billy maps out the killing of Sheriff Brady for Tom and Charlie.

22

wife Celsa can't quite conquer her desire to be seduced by Billy: the instinctual urge is stronger than even her fully developed sense of responsibility. The photographer at the wedding poses Billy with a rifle. It is, he carefully explains, not dangerous; but the use of it to lend glamour to the photograph sufficiently suggests the attractiveness of violence. Billy himself gradually becomes a figure of glamourised legend ('Killer of the West', etc.): in a clumsily explicit little scene Garrett's wife asks why so many people are coming into the town for Billy's hanging—'They've never seen anyone famous,' Garrett tells her. The point is made very strongly through Moultrie, the perverted southerner for whom Billy's messy and inglorious career offers a vicarious fantasy-fulfilment.

The episode at the party involving Joe Grant, the law enforcement officer touring to 'see how the amnesty holds', makes especially real the pervasive sense of the precariousness of the order. (Although the characters are quite distinct, the scene interestingly anticipates the humiliation of Hamer in *Bonnie and Clyde*). Grant is no monster: the character is created with such sureness of touch that the irony of the official upholder of order possessing those very traits that subvert it is not weakened by any implausibility. Grant cannot resist provoking Billy: he needs the glory of killing him to bolster his ego. And Billy, with his instinctive reaction against the man's pretensions, cannot resist playing with and provoking Grant. The notch Grant has marked in his gun to commemorate the man he has shot suggests again, in its pitiful self-importance, the glamour accruing to killing. The significance

of the episode, in which order is all but destroyed by violent impulses arising almost casually from commonplace self-assertiveness, is summed up in Pat Garrett's comment: 'One shot. One ten cent bullet and that's it.'

But the fullest realisation of the tensions underlying *The Left-Handed Gun* is perhaps to be found in the sequence of the shooting of Hill, the last of the four men, during Pat Garrett's wedding celebrations. The characteristically complex effect of the scene arises from our being sympathetically drawn to different characters and different sets of values simultaneously. All the thematic strands of the film come together in this scene, which must be seen in its context. The presence of Charlie, for instance, although he plays almost no part in the main action, is very important. His squirting of the wine, in the manner of the innocently homosexual horseplay that characterises the young men's relationship, brings into the scene the uninhibited and infectious spontaneity that has evoked so strong a response earlier in the film (for example, the horny toad joke on Billy's 'corpse', or the flour fight with the soldiers.) Yet it was Charlie's 'spontaneity' that made it possible for him to kill Moon when Billy, we feel, was going to spare him. Against this spontaneity, which Garrett never quite knows how to cope with (see his reaction outside the church after the flour fight), are set the social values of restraint and orderliness, embodied in Garrett himself and in the whole social setting: the scene opens with Garrett and his bride motionless amid a 'composed' group, from which the camera tracks back to reveal the wedding photographer timing the exposure. We are drawn to Hill, the potential victim, neither stupid nor wicked, who claims to the end, convincingly, that he believed the four were going to arrest, not kill, Tunstall (yet—it is a typically complex touch—Hill is the one we were shown actually cocking his pistol as Tunstall rode towards them). It is Hill who makes nonsense, finally, of Billy's simplified and absolutist morality: through him we understand so well how a basically decent man could be drawn into partial complicity in an evil action. Finally, there is Billy himself, and his uneasiness as soon as he knows Hill is present. To no extent do we endorse the killing of Hill, but this does not lead to a withdrawal of sympathy from Billy. For one thing, it is left an open question—which Billy himself clearly couldn't answer—to what degree the killing is a matter of conscious intention. Propped up for the photographer, with the harmless rifle in his hands, Billy watches Hill move away. It looks as if he may let him go. He would almost certainly have spared Moon. Hill has pleaded his case credibly, and stated that he would only use a gun if drawn on. (He is rebuked for interrupting and chivvied away by the indignant photographer: the touch of comedy adds to the complexity of tone and beautifully keeps in view the social values of the scene). Then suddenly Billy shouts to Pat Garrett. Is he desperately begging Garrett to restrain him, or issuing a warning that he can't allow Hill to get away, his inflexible desire for what he sees as 'cleanness'—the completing of the revenge—getting the better of his sense of the situation and the person involved? Clearly there is a confusion of both: Penn judges the ambiguity very exactly. Hill fires several times, wounding Tom in the stomach, before Billy retaliates, killing him. Pat Garrett's ensuing passionate denunciation of Billy elicits a very direct response without cancelling out one's sense of the scene's overall complexity. If its progress is from that first composed group, bride and groom outside the church surrounded by stable society, to the disorder of terrified children, sobbing, cowering women, dead and bleeding men, bridegroom convulsed in an indignation that fuses the personal and the social, we cannot forget that the collapse of order and security has been precipitated by instinctual drives closely related to those that evoke so positive a response elsewhere in the film.

In the latter part of *The Left-Handed Gun*, Billy is relentlessly led to confront the results

Still: The death of Tom (James Best).

of his obedience to half-comprehended urges: what he has done to Tom, to Charlie, to Hill and his widow, to Celsa and Saval . . . destroying not only his enemies (real and supposed) but his friends. Billy's friendship (a friend: 'something you see that you can't quite make out') is as disastrous as his enmity. The embryonic relationship with Tunstall (the last person in the world who would have wanted the revenge that is Billy's only way of expressing his gratitude and devotion to him) is kept present by means of a series of unobtrusive reminders: 1. The burning effigy of straw that separates the seduction of Celsa from the shooting of Moon (though, through its implications, it also connects them). Billy, leaving Celsa, passes it when it has become a charred skeleton. 2. Tom's death. Like Tunstall, he rides away from Billy over the crest of a hill towards the waiting bullets. 3. Billy's encounter with gipsies who help him and with whom he rests. The scene is interesting in

Still: Billy and the gipsies.

anticipating that of the Okie camp in *Bonnie and Clyde*, but is not in itself very successful: rather conventionally treated (the gipsies haven't the individuality that one expects from even the most transitory characters in Penn's films), and arbitrary, an emotional effect intellectually conceived, a mere gesture towards significance.

The image of the burning effigy is another matter. The immediate effect of dissolving straight to it from Celsa's capitulation is most unfortunate: it looks like the crudest 'flames of passion' symbolism. In fact, the image carries very complex suggestions and associations. In the scene with Celsa, Billy has burned his newspaper death notice and announced that he has come alive again. The burning of the effigy for the Easter celebrations carries obvious death-for-resurrection significance. When Billy passes, and touches, the charred remnants, there is clear ironic comment on *his* resurrection. Further, irrespective of any religious meaning (Penn is not a 'Christian' director, and the overall tone of the film encourages us to look at the image from a non-Christian standpoint), the blazing effigy suggests the universal delight in violence and destruction, thereby extending the significance of Billy's own violent tendencies. It carries its reminder of Tunstall, and of Billy's conversations with him, suggesting the ironic wrongness of Billy's deeds in relation to the man whose death they ostensibly avenge. More precisely, it reminds us of Billy's inability to look beyond what he immediately observes (his shrug in answer to Tunstall's 'Why do they do that?') to explore meanings and motives. Finally, with reference to the seduction of Celsa, the dissolve from blazing effigy to charred ruin anticipates the bitter, disheartening sequel to the seduction, at the end of the film. One could object that the image is too loaded with meanings for its significance possibly to be grasped; but it makes, I think, its emotional effect without its multiple associations needing to be consciously examined.

In the last stages of the film, after his escape from jail, Billy, finally isolated in notoriety, retraces crucial stages in his past and is forced by loneliness and pain into a partial self-realisation: the house from which Tom rode to his death, and where Charlie's death was brutally hastened by Billy himself; the gipsies, with their undefined reminder of Tunstall; Saval and Celsa, and the misery of Saval's realisation of his wife's infidelity. And there is Moultrie, with his photographs of Billy at Pat Garrett's wedding, and of Charlie dead ('You can see the wounds'), and his pulp fiction accounts of Billy's glorious career. The contrast between the legend (supported and admired by a whole society needing some vicarious glamour and violence) and the miserable human reality, offers the film's clearest anticipation of *Bonnie and Clyde*. But Billy achieves something Bonnie and Clyde (wrapped up in the myth they themselves, through Bonnie's poems, partly endorse and live on) never achieve: the whole film moves towards the slow gesture with which Billy, beaten to the draw by Pat Garrett, reveals that both hand and holster were empty. In effect a suicide, it is also a tragic victory, in the conscious acknowledgement it implies. Billy is, to resort again to W. B. Yeats, 'The unfinished man and his pain/Brought face to face with his own clumsiness.'

THE MIRACLE ■
■ WORKER

Of all Penn's films, *The Miracle Worker* is the most direct, the least ambiguous, in emotional effect, and this has led many people, quite understandably, to regard it as a comparatively simple, minor work and not enquire into it too deeply. (On the lowest level, there is an inbuilt intellectual tendency to distrust a film that makes one cry so much.) This directness of effect is certainly no illusion, but it conceals a great underlying complexity.

The extent to which one becomes aware of this depends partly on where one feels the centre of interest in the film to lie: in Helen Keller or in Annie Sullivan. The spectacle of the deaf and blind child struggling to burst out of her imprisonment is so moving, and the performance of Patty Duke so extraordinary, that—despite the fact that Anne Bancroft's performance is at least equally extraordinary—it is easy to focus attention on the recipient of the promised miracle rather than on its worker. A true reading of the film must, I think, start from the parallels insisted on, partly in the dialogue, partly visually, between the two.

About half-way through the film, Annie Sullivan looks out of the window to see Helen, arms outstretched, face uplifted, groping her way towards the house. Dissolve into one of Annie's memories which punctuate the action: she, in the horrific almshouse for the mentally and otherwise defective, gropes her way from the dim, gesticulating shapes of madwomen towards a group of officials, and cries out to them, 'I want to go to school'. As the image dissolves back to Helen, the two blindly groping figures are briefly superimposed: in Helen, Annie recognises herself.

Not only the connection it makes, but the whole emotional power of the image, is central to the film. The real subject of *The Miracle Worker* is not deafness or blindness, or even, centrally, teaching or communication, but the life principle itself: the way in which life energies, if they are sufficiently insistent, can drive through all barriers and obstacles to force an outlet, whatever harm is done them

Still: Helen (Patty Duke) gropes her way towards the house, in The Miracle Worker.

28

on the way. And Annie is at least as central to Penn's development of this theme (*movement* is perhaps a better word) as Helen. In Helen the movement is more obvious, and it is through her that the overwhelming immediate effect of the film is made. The penultimate sequence, in which Helen at last realises the connection between finger-spelt words and the objects they indicate, constitutes one of the most moving affirmations in the history of the cinema. What is conveyed is above all the ecstasy of suddenly breaking through

frustrations to the potential fulfilment of the most fundamental of human appetites—the appetite to know, to express, to communicate, the very principle of creativity. The Helen we see at the end of the film may still be deaf and blind, but she seems almost the least handicapped of Penn's protagonists: less, certainly, than Bonnie Parker and Clyde Barrow. She has, indestructibly, the desire for fullness of

Stills: below—Helen's moment of understanding at the pump; right—release.

life concentrated within her by the years of total darkness in an unusually pure and un-corrupted form. Like Annie in *her* prison, the experience has made Helen 'strong'. And the strength, one feels, has been bought at less terrible cost: the Helen Keller Penn shows us (it will be understood, I hope, that I am concerned here with the film as an autonomous work, not with its fidelity or otherwise to what really happened) has it in her to be a more complete human being than Annie Sullivan will ever be. We are moved in this sequence by more than Helen's or Annie's personal triumph: by the communicated intense joy in life. Camera movement and editing involve the spectator to the maximum in Helen's ecstasy; we turn from the film with a renewed delight in and wonder at our own existence.

Especially, there is the use of the simple and basic symbolism of water and earth, and the keys. Helen's breakthrough happens when the water from the pump runs over one hand as her other hand is held in Annie's: physical sensation and consciousness (the finger-spelling) are suddenly fused, becoming all but interchangeable. From water Helen passes to soil—understood, then rubbed ecstatically on the face—and from soil to tree: the elemental symbolism of fertility appropriately linked with the released joy in existence. The sim-plicity is almost diagrammatical yet so intensely felt that there is no possibility of its being found spurious; the images, with their characteristic physicality, convey that duality of response to direct sensation and to con-sciousness that is so central to Penn's art. The use of the keys is also very beautiful. Helen has previously taken them from the doors of the dining-room in which Annie locked her for their battle and has given them into her mother's keeping. Now she takes them from her mother's pocket and finger-spells 'Teacher', then takes the keys to Annie. Helen's intelligence (and she just missed being committed to an asylum for the men-tally defective) is expressed in her ability to make the metaphorical connection; but the abstract idea is here fused with the concrete and practical—the gift of the keys is the bestowal of trust, and the acknowledgement of a debt only at that moment understood.

The affirmation is quite unambiguous, and not in the least inconsistent: the positive feeling for life gives all of Penn's films some-thing of the effect of affirmation even when—as in *The Chase* or *Bonnie and Clyde*—their outcome is entirely pessimistic. But the affirmation of *The Miracle Worker* is not a matter of the simple optimism that a brief synopsis might suggest: it is an affirmation grounded in a sense of the complexities and confusions of human existence. Which brings us to Annie Sullivan.

It is convenient to begin at the end, with the very last scene, and ask why Annie is suddenly able, sincerely, to tell Helen that she loves her, when she has found it impossible to do so all the way through the film. A whole complex of inter-related answers quickly presents itself. For the sake of clarity I will tabulate them, and show how they are all firmly rooted in the film, and not the idle proliferations of a critic's ingenuity.
1. Before, Helen was an animal; now, she is a human being. This is, clearly, why her father is able to love her at last, and Annie herself made a connection earlier between her inability to love Helen and Captain Keller's.

This is the only reason not connected with Annie's personal psychology.

2. Earlier, Annie said, 'I don't even love her: she's not my child.' Helen's behaviour in the final scene shows that now she *is* Annie's child. In the previous sequence she recognised and accepted Annie as her teacher; now, by embracing her and lying in her arms, she accepts her as a mother.

3. But Helen is also Annie's in another sense. Throughout the film she has sought, and on occasion explicitly demanded, absolute power over her. She insists on this as necessary for Helen's development; but her manner suggests again and again that it is also a personal need of her own. Especially revealing is the

Still: Helen accepts Annie as a mother.

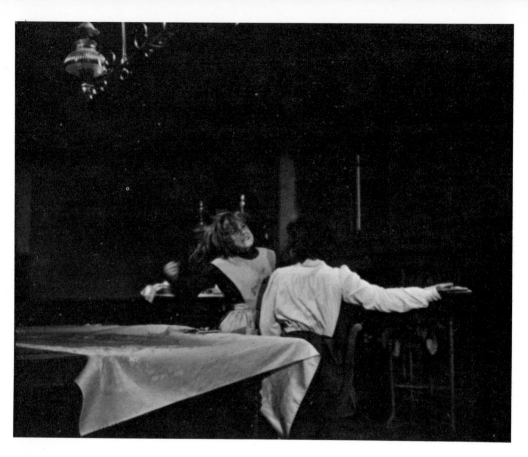

moment when, in reply to Captain Keller's suggestion that 'God may not have meant Helen to have the "eyes" you speak of', she defiantly asserts, '*I* mean her to.' Earlier, with Helen's half-brother James, she rejected the idea that she or Helen might give up, saying that 'giving up' was her idea of original sin. Annie, then, exempts herself from the supposedly all-reaching influence of original

Stills: the struggle to make Helen use a spoon, in The Miracle Worker.

sin, and frankly assumes the role of God. Even here, the motivation for this heroic arrogance is complex. Partly it is the result of the 'education' in the almshouse that has taught Annie to fight uncompromisingly for everything she has achieved. But it is also

compensation for the sense of disadvantage that seldom leaves her when she is in the company of adults. Her dark glasses do more than shade her eyes, they are a protection, to hold people at bay: James says to her at one point that she would not speak to him as she just has if she were not wearing her glasses. When she is behind her glasses she can fight. It is natural for someone chronically unsure of her ability to hold her own with people to compensate by seeking power where she has no sense of disadvantage. With Helen, Annie talks all the time in a relaxed, extrovert manner, often without her glasses on. The struggle to make Helen use a spoon comes across as at once an example of Annie's instinctive knowledge of what is necessary for Helen, and as a battle for power, with Annie driven on by a personal need. This ambiguity is fundamental to the total effect of the film.

4. To Annie, Helen imprisoned is Jimmy (Annie's brother) dead. The connection is made visually as Annie, beside the sleeping Helen, whose superimposed figure repeatedly recurs during the scene, remembers the time when she found Jimmy's body. Annie has strong guilt feelings about Jimmy—other memories have him pleading with her anxiously to stay with him, and in one she tells him she will leave him in order to go to school. Her responsibility to Helen is inextricably confused with her responsibility to Jimmy. She can't love the child, therefore, until the subconscious guilt is exorcised—until, that is, by saving Helen she resurrects Jimmy, which is another way in which Annie usurps the role of God, and one that suggests more clearly her need to do so.

5. But Helen, we have seen, is also Annie her-

Stills: communication through touch: Helen learns 'Bad girl' and 'Good girl'.

self. Annie's concern throughout is to triumph over her own disabilities—to prove that she can be a complete human being despite the ravages of her past experiences. She proves it, as it were, vicariously through Helen and loves Helen when it is proven.

These are, it will be plain, not so much five motives for loving Helen as five aspects, interconnected and interacting, of a whole complex motivation. They throw light, not merely on the end of the film, but on Annie's conduct throughout, and suggest, I think,

how central she and the film named after her are to Penn's work.

In fact, the title itself carries its small charge of irony. If we see a miracle in the film, it is surely Helen's moment of realisation at the pump; and it is made very clear that the realisation takes place because Helen remembers the sound for 'water' her mother taught her at six months. It is the first time she is able to connect objects with the concept of language. The 'miracle', then, is due largely to Mrs Keller, and to whatever has preserved

the memory of language, like an arrested seed, in Helen's subconscious through the years. Yet the crucial factor that makes the miracle possible has nothing 'miraculous' about it: Annie's passionately committed, single-minded struggle.

The action-processes of Billy the Kid and of Annie Sullivan might seem at first glance to be at opposite poles, since in total effect as in general intention the one is destructive, the other creative. Yet they have a great deal in common. Both start from a noble enough

concept, which one might define rather loosely as absolute justice in Billy's case, and educational vocation in Annie's. And in both cases the concept, considered as motivation, is real enough, but only a part, and perhaps the least decisive part, of the whole story. Beyond these concepts, both characters are partly blind:

blind to their own tangled motives (a word whose root sense of 'driving forces' is apt to slip away from it, but is particularly appropriate here). Annie's weak sight is doubtless in the factual data, but Penn uses it symbolically. The sense of someone driven on by intense personal needs he or she very imperfectly understands is as vivid in *The Miracle Worker* as it is in *The Left-Handed Gun*. Along with their blindness, Billy and Annie share an obsessive single-mindedness of purpose. Billy's sense of mission as he stands over Tunstall's coffin is paralleled in Annie's sense of one exclusive purpose: finding Helen not at the station to meet her, she tells Mrs Keller not to be surprised if, on the way to the Keller's house, she gets out to push the horse. Annie's assumption of the role of God recalls Billy's '*I'm* the law.' The affirmation of the one film and the tragedy of the other are but the two sides of a single coin.

The sense of creative forces struggling for freedom and expression is as potent in the presentation of Annie Sullivan as in that of Helen Keller: the conclusion of the film conveys, as well as Helen's release, an overwhelming sense of personal fulfilment for her teacher, a fulfilment rooted in Annie's whole past. We are left, nonetheless, with the impression of a woman whose strength is the corollary of terrible, and permanent, deprivations: the very intensity of her obsession, the concentration of her inner drives—her greatness, in short—relate to her unfittedness for normal life. But for Helen's recognition, she is isolated at the end as she has been, essentially, throughout the film. There is nothing sentimental or comforting in Penn's treatment of a subject that would seem to lend itself to every sort of indulgence. On the other hand, there is no sign of inhibition or embarrassment passing itself off as 'restraint': the emotional effect of *The Miracle Worker* is as pure as it is strong.

This is as good a place as any for a brief digression on critical method. I am perfectly aware of quoting lines from *The Miracle Worker* as if Penn, not William Gibson, had written them. I am perfectly aware that Penn is not credited with the scripts of any of his films, and that three of the five are adapted from plays by writers of some repute. I am also aware that the literacy and intelligence of the scripts contribute importantly to the films' success. Ideally, one would wish constantly to be introducing little qualifications and acknowledgements into one's text when quoting lines of dialogue. This is, however, a study of Arthur Penn, not of Gore Vidal, William Gibson, Lillian Hellman, etc. Penn's films reveal a strikingly consistent personality; even when one is aware of tensions or contradictions within his work, these come across as the expression of that personality. The films also suggest a conscious artist with the developed technique to express what he wants or needs to express. When the genuineness and intensity of a director's response are as evident as they are in *The Miracle Worker*, the film becomes his. These are Arthur Penn's films; the lines in a very real sense belong to him even if he didn't write them. One cannot always be acknowledging collaborators, but this doesn't imply unawareness or denigration of their contributions.

Still: Annie's fulfilment.

MICKEY ONE

Any anxieties one has about Penn are centred on *Mickey One*. It is not merely that the film is a failure—any artist is entitled to one failure out of five, or indeed to four out of five. One's anxieties arise partly from the particular nature of the failure, and partly from the fact that, of all Penn's five films to date, *Mickey One* was the only one made from completely free choice and with Penn in complete control, producing as well as directing. It is obvious enough, I think, from the close thematic continuity of the films, that Penn has never accepted subjects or scripts he hasn't *wanted* to do, but *Mickey One* was clearly, as a project, especially dear to him. Should one see it as an isolated mistake, or as the sort of film Penn would be making all the time if he could? There seems particular point in asking the question at a time when, after the world-wide box-office success of *Bonnie and Clyde*, Penn is presumably in a position to dictate his own contracts for a time (like Richardson after *Tom Jones!*). One can only hope that the artistic fulfilment represented by *The Chase* and *Bonnie and Clyde* has encouraged Penn to reject the possible line of development *Mickey One* signposts.

Not that *Mickey One* is undistinguished. If one saw it in isolation one would be tempted at first to suppose it the early work of an immature but talented young director; on second thoughts its remarkable assurance and perfection of technique would lead one to doubt this. There seems, indeed, a curious split between the immaturity of the overall conception and the extreme sureness and clarity of the execution. This technical assurance—the sense that Penn always knows exactly where to put the camera and why, that he knows unhesitatingly how to express each idea—at first seems the film's great virtue, but ends by rather telling against it. When one has taken the immediate impact and admired the general aplomb, one is left with the feeling of an enormous bluff, or confidence-trick. Given the film's half-baked and pretentious intellectual ideas, one can't help feeling that a few signs of doubt on Penn's part would

Still: Warren Beatty in Mickey One.

have been only decent.

Penn is a great American director. Though in an obvious sense more an 'intellectual' director than, say, Hawks or Hitchcock (the substructure of ideas seems nearer the surface in his films), he belongs essentially to the great tradition of the American commercial cinema —the significance of his work as a director arises from his concrete handling of concrete materials—action, plot, dialogue, stars, camera, decor—with intuition playing a vital and vitalising role. At the same time, Penn is clearly very much aware of the European cinema, the cinema of conscious intellectual ideas. To pass from Hawks to Antonioni, or vice versa, requires an act of adjustment that to pass from Antonioni to Penn does not. *Mickey One* has been called 'an attempt to make a European film in America.' It is Penn's attempt to deny the American side of his parentage. If one rejects one's ancestry one rejects, necessarily, a great deal of oneself; most of the richness and complexity of Penn's other films is absent from *Mickey One*. Thematically the film is central enough, and stylistically in many respects characteristic; but so much of what is most important in Penn is missing. It is curious that what is, on the surface, much the most obscure of his films should come across as also much the simplest.

Mickey One gives the impression of reversing Penn's usual method of working. In the other films, he starts from the particular and the concrete (in three cases out of the four, from an actual basis in fact) and discovers the universal by a process of exploration; in *Mickey One* he appears to have started from an abstract conception, a large general statement, and tried to *impose* the concrete on it,

Stills: above—Kamatari Fujiwara as 'The Artist'; right—Alexandra Stewart as Jenny.

and one is constantly aware of the imposition. The aim was clearly to make a film that would work on different levels simultaneously; the result tends to lurch from level to level with a confusion one cannot feel to be artistically resolved. Certain characters (e.g., the clown-artist with the dustbin lids, who seems to have strayed in from a Fellini film) appear almost exclusively symbolic; others (Jenny Drayton)

44

almost exclusively naturalistic. Penn fails to integrate them satisfactorily; the effect is particularly jarring in scenes where characters from different levels meet.

The interest of the film is two-fold: its thematic relatedness to Penn's other work, and the strength of some of its imagery. The protagonist of *Mickey One* is, like Billy the Kid and Bonnie and Clyde, a character with a fully developed popular image and a very uncertain sense of the relationship between this image and his real self: in this case, a successful (though not, to judge from what we see, very distinguished) night-club comedian. Successful, anyway, before the film starts. The credit sequence sketches briefly a fragmented life of luxury and irresponsibility. Near the end of it we see 'Mickey' (we never learn his real name) watching a man being savagely beaten up, then turning to make love to a girl while the beating continues in the background: the empty, self-ignorant, pleasure-seeking life surrounded by shadowy violence and menace: watching faces and unexplained phone-calls.

The end of the credits leaves Mickey alone with a scarf a girl has been sensuously dancing with slung over a drummer's stands by an empty dance-floor; and a sudden sense of indefinable guilt. 'They' are going to punish him for something—he isn't sure what. He tries to find tangible reasons for his punishment, for which an assessable penalty might be imposed, but Ruby Lapp, manager of the club where he works, suggests to him that he may now have to pay for *everything*. After flopping disastrously in his act, Mickey is seen running from Lapp out of a meat store-room hung with carcasses. Lapp shouts after him that he can't run away from 'them'—'You'll have to be an animal'. We are to see Mickey's enemies presumably, as both society (which has given him everything he wants in return for very little) and within himself. Lapp's parting call suggests that the enemy is the human consciousness itself. The film ends with Mickey's acceptance of his position, of the impossibility of escape and the necessity to confront whatever must be confronted, and this acceptance is led up to by one of the film's key lines. Jenny Drayton asks him, 'Are you frightened, Mickey?' and he replies, 'As long as I *live*.' The sense of continual precariousness and tension is part of what must be accepted.

A recurring problem is our uncertainty as to just how to take Mickey: he is so loosely defined. He is established firmly enough on a naturalistic level as a night-club entertainer, but Penn and his writer are not content to work consistently outwards from so concrete a basis, allowing universal implications to

Still: 'Are you frightened, Mickey?'

grow from a clearly defined situation. Instead, layers of symbolic meaning are imposed on the character. His relationship to the clown-artist, who takes Mickey to watch his art-work, happening or what-not, entitled YES, makes sense only if one sees Mickey as typifying The Modern Artist, with the sort of art YES represents as one of the possibilities open to him: already a heavy burden for an indifferent-to-mediocre comic to have to carry. Further, again and again in the film one cannot escape the suggestion that Mickey is Modern Man, and that Penn is tackling, head-on, big general issues such as Alienation.

The clown-artist is the film's most obvious weakness, the crudeness of the actor's performance only making manifest the crudeness of the conception. He is meant to represent a way of coming to terms with the modern environment by accepting and using it (his first appearance is in the middle of a used car dump, and at the end of the film he leads Mickey from the dump and the temptation of 'total death' to make *his* acceptance). But the purely symbolic nature of the character enables Penn to evade all the awkward questions he raises, about the conditions—moral, spiritual, psychological—necessary for making such an acceptance. There is also great doubt as to how seriously Penn takes him, and how seriously we are meant to. It seems a hopeful sign that Mickey looks (though even here one is none too certain) unimpressed by YES; but the fact that it is YES's creator who leads him back from the car dump at the end carries a strong (though

Still: the end of YES.

again imprecisely defined) symbolic significance.

Both the weakness of *Mickey One* and its thematic centrality to Penn's work can be illustrated by the sequence of Mickey's audition. Part-cajoled, part-tricked into going on stage to face unknown watchers (who may or may not be 'Them'), Mickey finds himself abandoned to an empty and darkened auditorium in which one dazzling spotlight (behind which are the auditors) mercilessly picks him out. Trapped, he tries to stall, makes weak, ineffectual jokes greeted by utter silence, sweats, panics, flees. The sequence suggests the inadequacy of the public mask to fulfil the private individual or provide any viable solution to his problems: as such, it offers a more explicit (and cruder) statement of one of the concerns of *The Left-Handed Gun* and *Bonnie and Clyde*. Yet for all the clarity (indeed, insistence) with which the intellectual idea is projected, one is uncomfortably aware of the confusion of levels in the realisation. Just what convention is operating? Are we watching naturalistic or symbolic drama? A comedian with a neurotic fixation about being persecuted, duped by a well-meaning night-club manager into an audition he isn't ready for? Or Modern Man on trial? If the first, then why does nobody know who is in the light booth and why does nobody try to find out? If the second, then how are we to adjust to it from the naturalistically explainable build-up between the manager and Jenny Drayton?

It is difficult to escape the sense of shallowness, the lack of those rich and complex resonances that distinguish most of Penn's work. The scene, for instance, where Mickey is set upon and beaten up by doormen from various night-clubs, each in different phoney national dress, makes no sense at all on the naturalistic level and conveys little beyond a general idea of our friend Modern Man in search of Identity being battered down by Appearances and False Values. Penn brings to it something of the direct physical impact that characterises his scenes of violence, yet this seems curiously irrelevant to the essentially abstract idea.

A 'symbolic' scene near the beginning has much greater force. Mickey throws himself off a train to find himself in a used car dump. Police officials are watching a reconstruction of a crime: the disposal of a body in a car being

Stills: left—'Is There Any Word from the Lord?'—Mickey's agent hides among hymn-singers; right—indefinable menace.

put through the destruction-by-compression process. The victim is related to Mickey through a reference to guilt about 'sources of revenue—his own or anybody else's.' He 'never made it in court . . . total death,' as the car is brutally crushed into a packed tangle of metal. Mickey runs, in terror, to be pursued by cranes and other machines involved in work of destruction, which seem bent on

Stills: above—'Total Death'; right—a new beginning?

crushing him. The sequence is shot and edited with characteristic physical immediacy, and here there seems less discrepancy between physical impact and symbolic meaning. The piles of wrecked cars provide a valid, if obvious, image for the impermanence,

50

machine-dominance and waste of industrial civilisation, and Mickey's fears of being overwhelmed and annihilated, with his very uncertain sense of identity (we have just seen him burn his social security card), are given fitting concrete expression.

One can see why Penn, a conscious and articulate artist with a most alive intuitive responsiveness to the 'feel' of modern life, its insecurities, its sense of latent, but only *just* latent, violence all round, should have wanted to make *Mickey One*. The film is useful as a crystallisation of certain of his leading concerns. One is very glad that, in his two most recent films, he has returned to his roots in the traditions of American narrative cinema, or to exploration, as opposed to explicit statement.

THE CHASE

Penn's first indisputable (one would have thought) masterpiece has in fact, in England at least, had somewhat meagre recognition, both from critics and general public. The director's intelligence informs every sequence: not merely a cerebral intelligence, but an intelligence in which emotion and intuitive perception have their essential roles, and in which the most rigorous clarity of vision is balanced (but not cancelled out or compromised) by emotional generosity. It is perhaps Penn's *completest* film. Not that it is necessarily to be preferred to *Bonnie and Clyde*, but it contains certain features excluded from the later film, which give it in comparison an extra dimension.

The Chase offers Penn's fullest portrayal of a particular society, the analysis leading to uncompromising condemnation, by implication, of money-based society in general. By the end of the film everybody from the highest (Val Rogers) to the lowest (the negro Lester) has been revealed as equally a victim. The essential nature of the society depicted (vividly particularized, yet carrying the widest possible implicit significance) is suggested early in the film by the scene in Val Rogers' bank: on the surface, an all-pervasive hypocrisy and wearing of masks; below it, the sense of frustrated and corrupted needs strong enough continually to threaten the brittle facade. The champagne toast to Val Rogers on his birthday, organised with obsequious efficiency by Damon Fuller, subtly conveys Val's position. The whole presentation of Rogers is a good example of Penn's quite unsentimental generosity. Rogers' 'image'— which he himself clearly accepts as real— of a thoroughly decent, responsible leading citizen, unassertive yet perfectly in control, is not *entirely* unrelated to the reality. Penn shows us a man by no means inherently vicious: his subtle corruptness, revealed gradually as the film progresses, is felt as something inherent in his position rather than in his nature. Because he is rich, he is universally respected; but the respect is for the money,

Still: Anna Reeves (Jane Fonda) and Jake Rogers (James Fox) arrange to meet.

52

not the man, hence false and precarious. As the champagne glasses are raised, the girl assistants smile their adoration: they are perfectly sincere, in so far as they believe they are really feeling something for the man. And the extent of Val's self-delusion is suggested by his evident pleasure at the tribute: he is as much trapped in money-values as anyone.

Even in the apparently ordered world of the bank, the tensions and frustrations underlying the social performance rise uncomfortably near the surface. Emily Stewart, wife of one vice-president, intermittent mistress of another (Damon), passes from taunting her husband Edwin with his ineffectuality to blatantly arranging an assignation with her not over-enthusiastic lover within her husband's view and only just out of earshot. Sexual intrigue associates itself easily with business intrigue: Emily's contempt for Edwin as a husband is scarcely distinguishable from her resentment at their not being invited to Val's party. The debasement of sex, and of personal relationships generally, is intimately connected with the all-pervading money-values. The scene culminates in Emily's insolently and publicly inviting Val to *their* party: the social masks are all but dropped. Throughout, the sense of explosive forces accumulating beneath the flimsy facade of propriety is very strong.

The social analysis is developed through the film's three simultaneous parties—Val's, the Stewarts', and the teenage party in progress next door to them. The three groups converge for the film's climax, where the social distinctions insisted on by the previous separateness break down in a general anarchy as all civilised standards finally collapse. The parties—two of them observed in great detail —offer superficial contrasts and underlying parallels. One notices repeatedly the inadequacy of the codes of social behaviour to cope with the violence latent in the personal relationships. Each party tends to move towards violent expression as suppressed energies force themselves increasingly to the surface. This is least obvious, necessarily, in Val's more formal and elaborate party, with its respectable ostentation. Even here, however, barely suppressed tensions are kept continually in view. It is a mark of Penn's seriousness that even the drunken middle-aged woman in the cowboy suit does not strike one as merely funny.

Take, for example, the incident of the formal announcement of college endowments, with its suggestions of an auction sale with guests outbidding each other to purchase status, and its complacent speech: 'We Americans must lead the world's ignorant masses. Only through books can man become free.' The irony is the more telling for the absence of any feeling of caricature: the pervasive money-vulgarity, the background of shallow, purely material 'culture', of false values and false pretensions, highlights the speech sufficiently. Mr Theodore Crane is giving 500,000 dollars to endow a dormitory for women. Cry from a giggling, semi-tipsy blonde: 'Why, you old goat. Are you up to it?' The sense of critical interaction here is typical of Penn: if the film satirizes the money-based self-importance of the donor, it certainly doesn't endorse the equally money-based vulgarity of the young lady—they are but two aspects of the same set of values. The ensuing

presentation to Val of a model of the college—
'One of the finest colleges that money can buy'
—conveys the implication that even the best
this society can show for itself is invalidated
by corrupt values.

The tension between surface and reality is
expressed even more strikingly in the personal
relationships. There is the pretence of married

Still: 'one of the finest colleges that money can buy'—Val Rogers (E. G. Marshall) and Jake with the model.

happiness by Val's son Jake and his wife: the
pretence of a pretence, rather, as Val isn't
even meant to be fooled by it. All he demands
is the merest show, and the pervading corruptness of values is suggested in the fact that the
show, even when he knows it to be a mockery,
can make him happy. Jake's is clearly a
money-and-status marriage: the 'decent' and
well-intentioned Val is behind it just as—being
the chief representative of money-power—
he is behind most of the corruption in the film.
In counterpoint with the scenes involving

Jake, his wife and his father at the party, we see Bubber Reeves flinging mud at a 'Val Rogers Properties' sign. The impotent and undisciplined action suggests the frustration of young people growing up in a money-orientated culture, feeling cheated, yet un-equipped to focus their resentment into any form of *purposeful* rebellion. Most of them, anyway, are too well off.

But if the harmfulness of values that ignore or deny the deeper human needs is very strongly felt in the film, so is their inability to hold in check the expression of such needs. When Jake learns that Bubber (his childhood friend, now married to the girl Jake loves) has escaped from prison, he leaves the party in-stantly, in the middle of his father's speech, to go to Anna. As he dashes away, Val is talking about 'responsibilities', and about his son's expected 'wonderful, rich, fulfilling life'. Fulfilment itself thus becomes a mockery, like the sense of 'responsibilities' that ex-presses itself in endowing a college and ruining the lives of those you love in the name of appearances.

The Stewarts' party, on the other hand, has the sort of atmosphere that passes for uninhibited, but is really a matter of acting out neurotic tensions without the possibility of exorcising them. In the party's rapid degeneration into an orgy of mock killing and mock suicide, accompanied by some real des-truction as a shoe 'grenade' hits the ice bucket and culminating in the firing of a real gun, we have reflected in miniature the movement of the whole film. Again there is a pervasive

Still: Jake with his wife (Diana Hyland) and father at the party.

56

sense of real needs unrecognised or strangled in a society that has set up material values as the ultimate ends. None of the characters at the party is equipped for finding any sort of valid fulfilment: all are circumscribed by the deeply entrenched attitudes of society as a whole. Their spontaneously erupting 'games', mostly jarringly malicious, necessarily express the cumulated violence within them, their hatred of each other and of themselves. As the Stewarts' party escalates into chaos, we are kept aware, through windows, of the teenagers' party in progress next door, reflecting the adults' in its air of imminent eruption. We have seen sufficiently by this time the world the young are growing up in, the values they are growing up to, the Americans who 'must lead the world's ignorant masses' in culture. Having come to investigate the pistol shot, the teenagers fall automatically into playing at Bubber Reeves, paralleling the violent games of their seniors. This extension to another generation, though only lightly sketched in, adds an extra dimension which takes on particular importance towards the end of the film.

The teenage party is also used to reveal new aspects of the adult characters. Damon Fuller's remark about 'liking them younger and younger', though disguised as a joke, comes across as somewhat more, in the context of his unsatisfactory marriage and half-hearted adultery, and gives a further suggestion of the pervasive corruption; Emily Stewart finds it rather thrilling. The incident

Stills: the Stewarts' party: above—Mary Fuller (Martha Hyer); below—Emily (Janice Rule) and the teenagers.

provokes the one moment of genuine feeling during the party when Edwin says, 'I wasn't thinking about things like that, Damon. I was thinking about myself at that age—the things I wanted and believed would happen.' It is typical of the characterisation in Penn's films that a man who has previously appeared largely contemptible should suddenly emerge here as the only person present at all worthy of respect.

Penn's characters sometimes tend towards caricature without ever quite slipping into it. The essence of true caricatures is that they are incapable of development, being exag-

Still: Mr Briggs (Henry Hull), who acts as a malevolent chorus, with his wife (Jocelyn Brando).

gerated features seen in detachment from any context of human wholeness or complexity. Thus it is a major weakness of Dickens' novels that so many of his characters cannot develop, they can only have arbitrary changes imposed on them by the author. Hence they become increasingly maddening at each reappearance, since all their author can do is put them through the same routine again: as they cannot develop, they cannot surprise us. This clearly isn't so of Edwin Stewart—or of Blanche Barrow, or even of Eugene and Velma,

in *Bonnie and Clyde*. If Edwin were mere caricature, it would be impossible for Penn to bring off (as he does, most touchingly) his moment of truth during the party, the genuineness of which makes his wife's ensuing public ridicule of him as a 'Saturday night philosopher' particularly brutal. Penn's near-grotesques have the same kind (if not degree) of complexity as his central figures; one is struck repeatedly by details of behaviour that at once surprise yet register as absolutely 'right', such as C. W. Moss's sudden nostalgic revelation that he and his family were 'Disciples of Christ', or Eugene Grizzard's laugh when invited to join the Barrow gang.

Set against this damning social analysis are the figures of Calder, the sheriff, and his wife Ruby: they and their relationship provide the film with its chief moral positives that place the other characters in the necessary perspective. Calder's mature poise serves as a touchstone by reference to which the others' lack of awareness can be measured. Through Brando's performance, Calder's integrity becomes a convincing presence in the film. His withstanding of all the pressures brought to bear to implicate him in the general corruption is never felt as a matter of empty heroics: he is a man who knows his own real needs, as the characters who surround him do not. Supported by a stable and fulfilling—if childless—marriage and a firm confidence in his own identity, he is able to move easily on any of the town's variously corrupt social levels without being contaminated. He copes with his social equals' vulgarity by turning it neatly back on them. Emily invites him in to the party: 'All you need to come to *my* party is a pistol and you've got one.' The tone of voice makes the sexual innuendo unmistakable. Calder coolly retorts, 'With all the pistols you got there, Emily, I don't think there'd be room for mine.' The whole town, from Val Rogers's vice-presidents to Mrs Reeves, assumes he is in Rogers' pocket; Rogers, when pressed by circumstances, reveals that he (unconsciously) assumes it too. Yet Calder acts firmly and consistently from his own personal centre, even when faced with the subtle moral blackmail of his debt to Rogers (who was responsible for getting him his position). Of central significance to *The Chase*—and, if *Bonnie and Clyde* can be taken as a reliable signpost, to Penn's whole future development—is the way in which Calder, who alone embodies an aware and fully adult social sense, is driven to reject in despair the society he has striven to hold together.

Brando's perfectly controlled performance has been generally recognised, the presence of Angie Dickinson as Ruby much less so. Miss Dickinson is a very considerable presence in every film she graces, but Hollywood has not always put it to the happiest use. Through her, Penn suggests something of what makes it possible for Calder to be what he is. The creation of the Calder-Ruby relationship is a triumph for Penn and his actors: there is nothing exceptional in the dialogue. What is conveyed is essentially a sense of commitment to each other, unemphatic, unostentatious, yet total. (Even here, their childlessness—unexplained, but we are left to presume it to be due to some physical disability or incompatibility—suggests the imperfectness of all existence). Particularly, Ruby's presence at three moments of climactic violence is crucial to the film's effect. Through her is kept present the touchstone of civilised and adult standards, against which we can measure the ignominy of Val Rogers' attempt to bribe Lester with 100 dollars and, when that fails, his vicious beating of him in a locked cell. The subsequent sequence of the beating up of Calder by a group of noteworthy citizens, in itself made uncompromisingly repellent, is

Stills: left—Emily invites Calder to her party; below—Ruby sees Val beating up Lester (Joel Fluellen).

given particular force by Ruby's presence on the other side (again) of the locked door: the impression of mutual trust and interdependence previously built up is so strong that what could have been a conventional scene of a woman screaming while her man is beaten up becomes almost intolerably moving. We experience it, as it were, through Ruby's sense of exclusion, her helplessness, her agonised uncertainty as to what, exactly, is being done.

Above all, there is Ruby's intervention when Calder, after the shooting of Bubber Reeves, finally succumbs to the by now ubiquitous violence, uselessly beating the killer with unrestrained and animal-like ferocity. It is the moment when the film's tragic intensity is most manifest, and Ruby's reaction is of key importance. It would be so easy, given the emotional pitch the film has by that time reached, to feel that Calder's descent to violence is justified: it could have been presented as a moment of release, like the traditional Western ending where the hero who has stood out against violence at last reaches for his gun, with the audience's full approval. Ruby's horror (combined of course with other factors in Penn's handling of the scene, such as the undignified messiness of Calder's actions) unequivocally prohibits such a reaction. It is also a moment where the social and personal threads become indistinguishable. The scene brings home to us at once the collapse of the social values on which Calder has until now taken his stand, his descent into

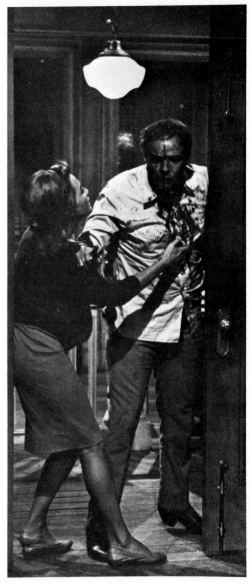

Stills: left—the beating up of Calder—Archie (Steve Ihnat) looks on; right—Calder staggers out.

everything he has stood against (made possible only by final disillusionment), and the personal horror of the loss of dignity and self-respect in a man of exceptional strength and integrity. As for the ending of the film, if one is to find any hope to qualify its terrible despair, it must be in the unobtrusive strength of Ruby's, 'Calder. Let's go. Come on.' The implied total defeat and disillusionment as far as society is concerned is slightly offset by our sense of the durability, at least, of one personal relationship.

But if the Calder-Ruby relationship gives *The Chase* its primary positive focal point, there is a strong secondary focal point which in many ways pulls against it, creating a powerful and disturbing moral tension in the film as a whole: the relationship of the three young people, Anna and Bubber Reeves and

Jake Rogers. The Calders represent a moral positive founded on a high conception of society, the young people an asocial morality based on personal loyalties. Calder is above all *conscious*, his actions (until his breakdown) are dictated by an enlightened awareness of the issues, an ability to stand back and shrewdly survey even while he is in the midst of events; the young people are above all spontaneous, acting from immediate impulses. To be able to respond to two partially opposed moral viewpoints simultaneously can be, if they are held in balance and with clarity, a sign of maturity and honesty rather than confusion.

Something of the film's attitude towards Bubber Reeves is suggested at the outset in the credit-title sequence, where pursued are shown against natural backgrounds while pursuers are shown against ominously huge and luridly lit industrial erections. The three young people are presented quite unglamourously and unsentimentally as confused, fallible and helpless, their actions involving them steadily deeper in disaster; yet for all their moral confusion, the comparative purity and naturalness of their responses to each other stand out vividly against the money-based responses of their more 'respectable' seniors. Jake, as Val's son, is necessarily the most trammelled of the three, but certain even of his actions—the refusal to leave the used car dump with his father, which marks his rejection of all Val stands for, his moment of final commitment—have considerable moral force. During the party, one notes the honesty of Jake and his wife with each other about their

Stills: left—Anna and Jake; right— Bubber Reeves (Robert Redford).

64

relationship, amid the surrounding hypocrisy —she asks him casually if he's going to see his 'friend' (Anna), and he as casually admits it.

The precise nature of the values embodied by this group of characters can be made clear with a few examples. The implicit overall attitude to the relationship between the three is itself very unconventional in its openness. Anna is Bubber's wife, Bubber is Jake's best friend, Jake and Anna are lovers. Yet the film imposes no moralistic attitude to this situation on the spectator. Also—and this is perhaps another way of saying the same thing —there is no schematising of the characters: they have to a marked degree the fresh and unexpected spontaneity of response one finds so often in Penn's people. Anna is in love with Jake, yet her reaction to the news of Bubber's escape is a spontaneous flow of sympathy towards *him*, an intuitive sense of need in someone she feels for. Her love for Jake is perfectly compatible with a sense of his weaknesses: she treats him (as in the incident of his gift of jewellery) always with a directness that ex-

Stills: left—Anna, Jake and Bubber reunited; above—the car dump.

presses her ability to trust and act on her own instinctive responses. During the search for Bubber, Jake tells her he's afraid he's going to lose her and says he wants to marry her. Instantly, like a rebound, she slaps his face: 'I've waited all these five years to hear you say that. It's just like you to say it at the wrong time.' We register the action as the expression of a natural, intuitive decency. When they find Bubber, instead of the expected explosion (various characters—Edwin Stewart, etc.— have been anticipating that Bubber will try to kill Jake), their earlier comradeship is not only preserved but strengthened. The desperation to which imprisonment has driven Bubber (whose urge to freedom has the instinctiveness of a trapped animal's) is a decisive factor here: 'When you're willing to die, nobody can make you do anything any more.' *In extremis*, the three discover an honesty and sincerity that entirely breaks down any ten-

67

dencies towards conventional or 'conditioned' emotional responses. Bubber's natural acceptance of Anna and Jake is above all an acceptance of natural impulses. Society understands only its own conditioned responses: hence the assumption that Bubber will kill Jake, and the assumption that Calder will support Val Rogers. The final condemnation of money-power comes most beautifully, and spontaneously, from Bubber Reeves. When he learns of Val Roger's offer of a car and a free escape, everything smoothed over, he exclaims, 'He can do *that*? What a world!' Here, then, is the film's secondary positive moral-emotional pole; the unorthodox 'natural' morality the three evolve carries great weight in the context of the depiction of the breakdown of conventional, artificial morality. The tension between the two poles can be suggested by reference to another example in the film of an absolutely natural, spontaneous reaction: Calder's beating of Bubber's killer.

It is the implications of this secondary positive force that Penn explores in *Bonnie and Clyde*. The relationship of the two films is extremely interesting. One knows, of course, that in Hollywood accident or extraneous factors can play a large part in what looks like a director's development; that the subject of *The Chase* was not entirely of Penn's free choosing, and that *Bonnie and Clyde* had already been offered to other directors (including, rather appropriately, Jean-Luc Godard) before Penn undertook it. Nevertheless, one cannot resist seeing a logical connection between the defeat of Calder and *Bonnie and Clyde*, in which a Calder has no part to play: one could almost say that Calder's defeat makes *Bonnie and Clyde* and the line

Penn explores in it inevitable.

The climax of *The Chase* offers a terrifying picture of social breakdown in which all the varied threads of the film are drawn together. The setting of the wrecked car 'graveyard' takes us back to *Mickey One* and 'total death', but here gains strength from being used dramatically where in the earlier film it was exclusively symbolic. Val turns up to save Jake, then the guests from the Stewarts' party appear, then the teenagers, as the news of Bubber's whereabouts spreads. As the ubiquitous violence explodes (literally, with fireworks and blazing wheels) all round, we watch Val increasingly losing control: ultimately, the power of money evaporates as frustrated instinctual urges fulfil themselves in destruction. The treatment of the scene is so convincing in terms of character that it is only afterwards one realises how close we are, here, to allegory. The condemnation of society is implied in the confused ambivalence of the teenagers' responses: Bubber becomes half folk-hero, half scapegoat, glamourized and hounded, at once a symbol of rebellion and a necessary victim on whom violence can be unleashed with at least some show of social righteousness. What they can't see him as is a human being, one of themselves. We see the beginnings of a Bubber Reeves myth ('Remember my sister?' a girl calls yearningly through the car window as he is driven to jail) that takes up one of Penn's favourite themes. Only here, at the moment when Bubber seems in danger of vanishing beneath his own legend, do we learn that he has a name (Charlie) other than the childish nickname; almost immediately after which he is shot *Still: Anna in the car dump.*

Stills: above left—Archie kills Bubber; above right-Calder surrenders to violence; right—defeat and departure.

down on the jailhouse steps. The sense of violence as an epidemic spreading with alarming and uncheckable speed is greatly strengthened by the fact that Bubber's killer is a man who has hitherto remained on the periphery of events, more spectator than participant, seemingly one of the least given to active violence.

Incredibly, some critics attacked *The Chase* when it came out in England for its emphasis on violence. Violence is a subject that an artist who is intuitively and intellectually alive to the world in which he exists can scarcely avoid today; and if there is a more responsible treatment of it anywhere in the cinema, I have yet to see it. In insisting on the topicality of the film, I am thinking of more than the clear reference to the killing of Lee Harvey Oswald in the shooting of Bubber Reeves. Although

everything in *The Chase* is so vividly particularised, it would be a mistake to see it merely as a portrait of a localised society. (Whether or not it is a faithful portrait of contemporary Texas is a matter quite outside my competence, and seems to me anyway of trifling importance. The society of *The Chase* can be taken as completely fictitious: its relationship to the fundamental realities of modern civilisation remains unaffected.) It seems to me to offer tragic comment on the present world-spirit: the sense that the traditional social values of western civilisation have been worn so thin that they are no longer capable of holding the forces they have rendered the more explosive by suppressing. The film captures unnervingly that feeling of latent or erupting violence which has doubtless a particular relevance to the Deep South but which is to some extent in the air we all of us breathe.

BONNIE & CLYDE

Besides being the culmination of Penn's work to date, a film of marked and consistent individuality in which every shot bears the director's signature, *Bonnie and Clyde* is also the culmination to date of the long and honourable tradition of the gangster film. The influence of the New Wave has, clearly, played a part in determining its precise nature. Nevertheless, without denying the importance of the influence, it is necessary to insist that there is nothing in *Bonnie and Clyde*, stylistically, technically, thematically, which was not already implicit in *The Left-Handed Gun*. The New Wave's example of spontaneous inventiveness seems to have acted as a releasing rather than determining influence. Confronted by Penn's use of slow motion, of special photographic textures (the reunion with Bonnie's mother), of free intercutting of events separate in time and space (the car chase repeatedly interrupted by 'cameos' of policeman and, farmer giving their reactions to the robbery), one does not think of imitation (as one does, for instance, with the speeded-up motion and 'free', 'lyrical' tracking-shots of trees, etc., in Richardson's *Loneliness of the Long Distance Runner*): Penn's 'New Wave' liberties work on too deep a level, and are too essentially inherent in the style and mood of an entirely coherent and consistently 'felt' whole.

It is legitimate, in view of this cross-fertilisation, to place *Bonnie and Clyde* in a tradition of the gangster film (using the term very loosely) that includes, not only *Scarface* and its forerunners, neighbours and successors, but also *Breathless* and *Pierrot le Fou* (but not, for example, the 'forties Chandler/Hammett cycle and its derivatives). Leaving aside all question of different kinds of gangsters (and whether the term 'gangster' is in some cases applicable at all), one can see a far more essential link between these films: a link whose nature one can point to by adducing further a film such as Hawks' *Monkey Business* (not a gangster film in any sense) and Shakespeare's Falstaff and Cleopatra. We are brought face to face very quickly with the immorality

Still: Clyde (Warren Beatty).

of *Bonnie and Clyde*, which I shall not attempt to deny; immorality, not from the point of view of repressive bigotry, but of any sensible social morality. For all the blood and pain, for all that we see the protagonists meet peculiarly horrifying deaths and are shown quite unequivocally that 'Crime does not pay', the film is far more likely to encourage spectators to be like Bonnie and Clyde than to encourage them to be conforming, 'responsible' citizens in society as it exists. The Bonnie and Clyde of Penn's film, however many banks they rob, however many men they kill, remain attractive and sympathetic characters: plainly, the most attractive and sympathetic in the film. Obviously, the intense identification audiences feel with the characters is a major factor—*the* major factor—in the film's immense box-office success: a success whose sociological implications become even more frightening when one sets it beside the comparative commercial failure of *The Chase*, a film equally violent but characterised by a very different (superficially, all but contradictory) moral attitude. We recognise that Bonnie and Clyde *have* to be shot down, just as we recognise that Prince Hal *has* to disown Falstaff and that Cleopatra *must* be defeated and trapped into suicide by Octavius Caesar. Yet Bonnie and Clyde, Falstaff and Cleopatra dead continue to be more attractive and sympathetic than Texas Ranger Hamer, Hal or Octavius living. Why? Because, even in death, they are more completely alive, and it is the insistence of life within them—of spontaneous, socially amoral and subversive energies—that makes it necessary for them to be destroyed. That is

Still: Bonnie (Faye Dunaway).

why one can speak, in these cases, of the artists' *tragic* sense.

The essential link of which I spoke lies in the ambivalence towards the protagonists and their behaviour, an ambivalence felt by the artist and communicated to the audience. Doubtless what I am saying is partly that Penn 'romanticises' Bonnie and Clyde, but I am saying it without the intent of condemnation the term usually implies. The lives and characters of the real-life Bonnie Parker and Clyde Barrow may have been, for all I know, entirely grubby and squalid. Penn uses them (as Hawks used, much less attractively, Al Capone/Tony Camonte, and as Godard uses Michel Poiccard) as representatives of a spontaneous-intuitive aliveness that society even at its best can contain with difficulty or not at all: an aliveness that expresses itself in the overthrowing of restrictions, in asocial, amoral freedom and irresponsibility. We all respond to it; or if we don't, we might as well be dead.

Immediately, of course, qualifications have to be made to this account: it is, I think, a measure of the greatness of *Bonnie and Clyde* that whatever statements one makes about it, qualifications immediately spring to mind, urging one to more precise and more complex definition. The term 'romanticise' has come to carry overtones of the Women's Mag. novelette, and the most cursory glance at Penn's presentation of his gangsters will show how inapposite any such suggestions are here. Perhaps the word can be restored to something of its original dignity by relating it to the Romantic tradition itself—the movement that in English literature begins with Blake and has its last great explosion in D. H. Lawrence, and whose main source of vitality and impetus has consistently been the belief in the importance —even the sacredness—of the spontaneous-intuitive side of man's nature. *Bonnie and Clyde's* final images of the two white-clad bodies writhing in a progressively blood-soaked agony beside the white car, with their overwhelming sense of desecration, the over-tones of man's defilement of nature (machine-guns glinting metallically amid foliage as flocks of disturbed birds flutter away), the feeling of ritual conveyed by the slow motion, are above all 'Romantic' images, in the main-stream of the Romantic tradition. (They are also, such is the film's complexity, ironic, the irony counterpointing and intensifying rather than destroying the 'Romanticism'). This 'Romantic' tendency is not new in Penn: one recalls the credits of *The Chase*, with their industrial/natural opposition, and the scene where Calder and Ruby, driving away from Val Rogers's party ('What the hell were we doing there?'), see a wild horse bound across the road in front of the car, an image of natural freedom that relates to Calder's desire to return to farming and immediately prompts him to say, 'We'll make it'.

Comparison with *Scarface* is instructive. One can state one essential difference by saying that in Hawks' film there is a greater distance between the spectator and the pro-tagonist (not, I think, explainable in terms of the film's having dated—it is in fact still remark-ably fresh and vigorous. We are introduced to Tony Camonte as an ape-like shadow on a wall, and this image sets the tone for the whole presentation of him. The gangsters' irrespon-sibility and audacity certainly evoke a strong response—the violence is more consistently exhilarating than in *Bonnie and Clyde* because the exhilaration is given much less counter-balance in terms of our awareness of suffering —but total identification is impossible be-cause we are consistently made to feel the gangsters as arrested or stunted human beings. Penn's presentation of *his* gangsters is quite clearly not a matter of uncritical adulation—if 'Romanticised' they are never glamourised—but they are not diminished as Hawks' are: we never feel superior to Bonnie and Clyde. Partly the distinction is stylistic: where Hawks keeps his characters for the most part in medium- or long-shot, Penn brings us physically so close to his that it is difficult to remain detached. When Bonnie beats on the cross-bar of the bed at the beginning of the film, the camera is as close as it can be in front of the bar and Bonnie's face as close as possible to her fist: we are not allowed to look at her frustration objectively, from a distance, but at once *her* frustration becomes the epi-tome of all *our* frustrations. Hawks' camera for the most part records: its objective move-ments are dictated by the desire for maximum clarity. The free, impulsive movements of Penn's camera catch the spectator up very directly in the movement of the action—the *emotional* movement as well as the physical. There is also the simple historical point that Penn is able, with the relaxation of censorship, both official and unofficial, to present Bonnie and Clyde far more intimately than Hawks could risk in his depiction of Tony Camonte (the incestuous tendencies of Tony and his sister had to be presented in a way that would pass for a 'beautiful relationship' with the simple- or conventional-minded).

The other major difference between *Scar-face* and *Bonnie and Clyde* might seem at first

glance to pull the other way, against closer identification with Penn's protagonists. The potential (and ostensible—see the foreword) subject of *Scarface*, the outrages committed against Society, is in fact scarcely treated by Hawks at all: 'Society', for all the urban settings of restaurants, hospital, theatre, is never felt as a major presence in the film, which is almost exclusively concerned with

Still: Bonnie and Clyde.

gang wars, treated by Hawks as kids' games played with real bullets. Penn's film, on the other hand, if one adds up all the details and the incidental characters (who, as well as being vividly individualised with an extraordinary sureness, economy and variety of touch, are representative figures), offers a

77

satisfyingly inclusive depiction of a society, complex and non-schematised. To this portrait contribute: the scene with the ejected farming family at the house closed by the bank; the background implied by the character of Blanche Barrow; the escapist cinema of the 'We're in the money' number, standing out brutally from the 'depression' background; the riverside camp of poverty-stricken outcasts; Bonnie's mother and relatives; the grocer with the meat-cleaver; Hamer the Texas Ranger; Eugene and Velma; C. W. Moss's 'Daddy'; the farmer in the held-up bank whose money Clyde doesn't steal; the middle-aged waitress in the café just after

Stills: shooting practice outside the house closed by the bank.

Bonnie and Clyde's first encounter, and Bonnie's own job as waitress; the bank assistant who gets shot in the face and the cashier in the bank that has closed down. But we are far here from the social values implied in the sequence of Pat Garrett's wedding in *The Left-Handed Gun*: as in *The Chase*, we are left with the impression of a social 'order' so corrupt as to be scarcely worth defending. In opposition to this, there is developed in the course of the film through the growth of the characters—particularly the women—a positive yearning and need for the stability their lives so pathetically lack.

It may be objected at this point that I am ignoring the film's very acute 'period' sense. I do so deliberately. Not because I don't think it important: one could write an essay on Penn's care in reconstructing the details and atmosphere of time and place in this and other films. But the specific is but one way of approaching the universal, necessary to many artists. Penn's immersion in the realistic details of a particular epoch or locale clearly acts as a valuable release and stimulus for that freedom and spontaneity that characterises all his work. Even *Mickey One* intermittently succeeds in so far as the physical particularities of the direction triumph over the abstract generalities of the script. What one should guard against in *Bonnie and Clyde* is the tendency to distance the film; to make it 'safe', by seeing it as a period piece: 'That's what things were like in certain areas of the United States in the 'thirties'. The limitations of such a reaction are sufficiently demonstrated by the extreme spectator-involvement the film provokes among audiences here and now. The photographs and song of the credit titles evoke a period and a specific reality very exactly, but they also evoke a yearning that is timeless, a permanent part of the human condition.

Bonnie and Clyde are themselves the products of the environment they reject, their vision of life's potentialities circumscribed by the values and attitudes of the society they outrage. The limitations of their backgrounds make it impossible for their rebellion to take any positive, constructive form—impossible, even, to deserve the name 'rebellion', which implies deliberate action and an awareness of the issues quite at odds with the casual and unreflecting drift into crime Penn depicts with an effect at once comic, frightening and exhilarating. The treatment is very complex: Penn is at pains to remove any false glamour accruing to the characters, but even as he prevents them from becoming possible fantasy-fulfilment figures of any crude or obvious kind, he develops them as characters who evoke a strong positive response. The concept of the folk-hero is important here: while examined in ways that would seem deliberately to undermine any tendency towards the creation of myth (with, indeed, the kind of ironic contrast between myth and reality pointed much as we would expect from the director of *The Left-Handed Gun*), Bonnie and Clyde retain to the end the essential qualities of the heroes and heroines of folk-ballads: they live from their spontaneous impulses, not from any codified morality or any reasoned or conscious attitude. The very title of the film encourages this view of Bonnie and Clyde;

Photograph: Penn directing Warren Beatty and Faye Dunaway.

so, of course, does the banjo-music used consistently to intensify the sense of spontaneity and exhilaration.

The credit-sequence provides an admirable starting-point for the film, with its juxtaposition of actual photographs (a drab reality) and the song 'Deep in the arms of love' (debased romantic dream). It implies at once the need to transcend or escape from commonplace reality and the lack of any spiritual or intellectual training for finding a *valid* alternative. The quite unglamorous commonness

Still: the exhilaration of violence—Bonnie and Clyde with C. W. Moss (Michael J. Pollard, left) and Buck Barrow (Gene Hackman).

of Bonnie and Clyde is emphasized throughout the opening, from that first big close-up of lips to which lipstick is being heavily and crudely applied. Yet from the start one is made aware of an underlying aliveness, an innate sensitiveness of response, especially mutual response. Each immediately sees through the other's pretensions—Bonnie knows that Clyde hasn't the money to buy his dinner, let alone a car; Clyde can unerringly 'place' Bonnie as 'a waitress'—yet this in no way lessens the instinctive respect and affection they feel for each other. They react intuitively to each other's human reality—the shallowness of the pretensions doesn't matter a bit. This whole opening sequence—indeed, like everything else in the film—is marvellously judged. The spectator is caught up, delighted, in the freedom of the characters' behaviour; at the same time, there is already implicit the sense that this delightful and infectious spontaneity, unhampered by any awareness beyond that of the moment, at once involves them in a course of action both destructive and self-destructive from which it will be difficult to retract.

At first Penn involves us in the simple exhilaration, to which we surrender almost as unreflectingly as the characters: after the first robbery, undertaken with an entirely disarming casualness, the stolen car sets off in wildly uncontrolled zigzags to the joyous accompaniment of banjo-music as Bonnie lavishes kisses and caresses on her new-found man. The process whereby we are made to confront and live through the full implications of the total irresponsibility we have so happily surrendered to is calculated with great exactness; though one scarcely thinks of calculation while watching a film that flows so freely. From the reckless gaiety of the first robbery, each act of violence is made to convey a slightly intenser charge of doubt, anxiety, and finally revulsion. The incident at the deserted farmhouse, where Clyde, the ejected farmer, and the negro, Davis, take turns in shooting the bank notice and then the windows, begins by developing a feeling of exhilarating defiance of unjust authority and an unjust social order, and with it a sense of growing comradeship between the three men that makes nonsense of differences of upbringing or race (though even here the sense that it is the farmer's own home that he is helping shoot to pieces gives a counterbalance of uneasiness: nothing in Penn is simple). But the farmer's silent reaction to Clyde's proud 'We rob banks'—clearly not the response Clyde wanted—suddenly places Bonnie and Clyde in a different category. The effect is ambivalent, like so much in the film: we can feel the farmer as conforming, through cowardice or conventionality, to the social order that has ruined him; we can also see implicit Bonnie and Clyde's whole future as outcasts not only from established society but from any kind of normal existence. There follows the attempted robbery of the bank that has closed down, which culminates in an almost identical action of shooting windows; but this time the cashier cowers in terror from a gun that might be turned on him: we feel a subtle modulation of mood from the previous incident. The next act of violence—Clyde stealing the groceries—culminates in the smashing of a man's face (the grocer who attacks Clyde with a meat-cleaver), and for the first time we are confronted with the fact of physical suffering (wounds always look more painful in Penn's films than in almost anyone else's). The next robbery, of the bank, ends with the horrific shot of the bank assistant's face blasted by Clyde's gun point blank through the car window. Throughout this carefully graded escalation of violence the sense of exhilaration and spontaneity is maintained, so that an extreme tension is set up in the spectator: a simultaneous involvement in and repudiation of the robbers' actions. Certainly, we are too much 'with' Bonnie and Clyde ever to extricate ourselves from complicity in their actions or participation in their inevitable punishment. The casual, unaware way in which they drift into a situation which, from the moment of the first killing, is hopeless, is closely reflected in the way the spectator is trapped into this sense of complicity.

Counterpointed with this development of the public aspect of Bonnie and Clyde's careers—the actions that directly affect society—is the development of their private relationship; through the pattern of alternating development Penn suggests the interaction of

Still: the death of Buck; Blanche (Estelle Parsons) restrained by police.

the two. The stress laid on Clyde's impotence is of course a further aspect of the deglamourizing process: it is not a characteristic common to many folk-heroes. On the other hand, it greatly aids the corresponding humanizing process: Clyde's sexual difficulties are but an extreme form of what a great many young men pass through in our society, and they enable Penn to comment ironically on another contemporary myth, that of complete sexual normality (in the psychological sense) being 'normal' (in the other sense). The contrast between the intimate scenes we have witnessed and the image Clyde (with Buck's encouragement) presents to his brother, strikes sympathetic chords in more spectators than might be ready to admit it. It's important that the audience is already sufficiently caught up in the exhilaration of total irresponsibility before the revelation of Clyde's impotence, to be carried through it without the risk of alienation: we never, I think, become tempted to regard Bonnie and Clyde as just a couple of psychotics: as well as having their own individual and complex life as fully realised characters, they are an extension of impulses common to us all, their abnormalities an extension of abnormalities widespread in our civilisation. They are, as Bonnie so poignantly tells Eugene and Velma in the car, 'just folks, just like us'.

A clear connection is established between Clyde's impotence and his criminal tendencies. His gun is a phallus-substitute: as he lets Bonnie fondle it during their first meeting, holding it out to her surreptitiously, the matchstick in his mouth jerks excitedly up and down. Later, when they try to make love, after Bonnie has failed to rouse him she is left

Still: first encounter.

pathetically caressing the revolver. The symbolism sounds crude in description, but isn't in execution: the treatment is too natural and unforced, and, in the earlier scene at least, too good-humoured. Bonnie robs with Clyde as a substitute for intercourse: it is at least *one* exciting thing they can do together.

The essential beauty of Bonnie's character —beneath the apparent shallowness, the tartishness, the impression given of previous promiscuity (her behaviour towards Clyde in the early stages of their relationship suggests that she has had plenty of erotic experience)— emerges as her attachment to Clyde deepens. Her first reaction to his impotence is one of bitter indignation: she feels intensely humiliated when he repels her (overwhelming) advances. After the first killing, he gives her the chance to turn back while she still can, and she commits herself to him irrevocably by refusing: the mutual respect and tenderness revealed results in his attempt to make love to her, partly as an act of gratitude, partly because he wants to be able to. Her reaction to his failure shows a sensitivity that clearly marks the extent to which the relationship has released an emotional capacity in Bonnie of a depth previously unguessed at. One of the principles of the film is that as their personal relationship gets more valuable, so their public situation becomes more hopeless, in fairly close ratio.

Two linked episodes particularly emphasize

Still: attempted love-making.

both the 'normality' of the gangsters and their irremediable isolation from any form of 'normal' existence. The most striking is the reunion with Bonnie's mother; the other is the incident that leads up to and indirectly precipitates it, the 'kidnapping' of Eugene and Velma. The earlier scene is an admirable instance of the flexibility and complexity of Penn's work at its best. Interpretative criticism has an inherent tendency to schematise, and it is precisely scenes like this that can easily become coarsened in the process of analysis. What looks at first like a very funny caricaturing of respectability—to the advantage of the uninhibited gangsters—is in fact much more: a mutual interaction of the two sides that subtly modifies one's attitude to both. Penn's handling of the scene goes far beyond any facile pointmaking, flexibly exploring the complex potentialities of the situation. The key line is perhaps Bonnie's 'You're just folks, just like us,' which has an immediate irony, coming from her: according to convention, it is Eugene and Velma who could claim to be 'just folks'—at the mercy of brutalised gangsters. Yet the irony itself works complexly: it's already established that the gangsters are (comparatively) natural and uninhibited, where Eugene and Velma seem slightly freakish: we are made suddenly to see conventionalised society as the more 'abnormal'. As the scene progresses, exposure to the gangsters' 'naturalness' gradually relaxes the two, so that they do indeed become 'just folks, like us'—positively human. Eugene loses most (not quite all) of his near-blubbery panic, discovering an unexpected camaraderie (his arm round Buck's shoulder), until his laughter at being invited to join the Barrow gang shows that a part of him is almost temp-

Still: the field of corn-cobs.

ted; Velma is betrayed by the relaxation into a moment of spontaneous honesty—she gives away her real age, before a somewhat appalled Eugene. On the other hand, as their 'respectable' facade lapses, we are aware that the gang are putting on something of a facade of their own. The previous scenes had shown tensions between them (especially Bonnie and Blanche); for Eugene and Velma, their very naturalness has something about it of an act: they are getting it both ways, being the terrifying Barrow gang yet at the same time at pains to present an image of 'just folks'. If the incident modifies, for a minute or two at least, Eugene and Velma, it has a more lasting effect on Bonnie. When she learns that Eugene is an undertaker, she promptly, in a moment of terrible premonition, has them turned out of the car. The next thing we know of her is her hysterical run (the next day) through the field of parched corncobs (a beautiful, disturbing image, drained of bright colour, with cloud-shadows sweeping irregularly across), and her sudden desire to see her mother. It is clear, I think, that this doesn't result merely from Eugene's being an undertaker, though that is felt as immediately precipitating it: Bonnie has made momentary contact with social stability, and Eugene and Velma, humanly inadequate as they are, have brought home to her, subconsciously, all that she has

Still: After being wounded in a police ambush, Bonnie and Clyde convalesce at the home of C. W. Moss's father.

missed. The premonition of inescapable and perhaps imminent death intensifies the sense of loss.

Hence the scene with Bonnie's mother is given the atmosphere of a dream, by the hazy photography, by the unobtrusive moment of slow motion as a child rolls down a bank. The setting is a waste ground, a no-man's-land between society and outlawry, the only place where the two can momentarily touch. Bonnie's mother and sister are not in the least sentimentalised. With the mother, indeed, Penn sketches in with his characteristically assured economy one of those old people who are among the typical products of a basically rural society overtaken by the values of the modern world: a woman of little awareness, bewildered by the world around her, with a confused sense of her own identity and the relations between things, her emotional capacity stifled, neither very loving nor very lovable. Yet he also gives her moments of merciless if limited clarity and insight which make her cruelly aware of Bonnie and Clyde's precariously self-deluding fantasy of being able to settle down when they want to.

Despite the total lack of idealisation of Bonnie's family and the social background they imply, Bonnie's nostalgia is painfully real and meaningful to us. There is a beautiful unobtrusive moment where a small boy playfully beats Clyde with a leafy spray and a relative nervously makes to stop him: the man he is playing with is a notorious multikiller. Even Clyde has a slightly surprised look, as if caught for an instant between his public image and his private self. In the scene a mere casual 'bit of business', it poignantly suggests at once the humanness of the man and the hopelessness of his situation—again the characteristic ambivalence that makes *Bonnie and Clyde* so disturbing. We share Bonnie's nostalgia, and yet the dream-like atmosphere works directly on the spectator. Seen from the spontaneous 'life' of the Barrow gang, it is society that seems unreal.

Much of the poignance of the film's later developments arises from the gradual discovery of incompatible needs within Bonnie

Still: C.W. and his 'Daddy' (Dub Taylor).

and Clyde's close, intuitive attachment. As Bonnie's commitment to Clyde deepens, so her need for stability develops; for Clyde, on the other hand, the public image of desperate bank-robber and killer is a need at least equally strong. He can't live without the assumed identity, even if the identity is false, leaving out of account (indeed, denying) everything that is most important in the human being, very much as Michel Poiccard in *Breathless* needs the Bogart gangster persona whose adoption limits and ultimately

destroys him. Is the overcoming of Clyde's impotence too abrupt for psychological verisimilitude? It is a development that could perhaps have been prepared more thoroughly. Nonetheless, the complex of factors behind it makes it convincing in retrospect, however abrupt in presentation. For the first time since their meeting, Bonnie and Clyde have found, under the equivocal protection of C.W.'s ever-loving 'Daddy', something resembling the security of normal life. Previously, Clyde has tried to keep other people around as safeguards against the possibility of further intimacy between Bonnie and himself. During their first night together he slept outside; then C.W.'s snoring presence in the same room made it possible for him to share Bonnie's bed (a poignant and desolate wordless scene with Bonnie lying awake in sexual frustration while Clyde, turned from her, pretends to sleep); then he surrounds himself with Buck and Blanche, until Bonnie asks, 'Don't you want sometimes just to be alone with me?' ('I feel we're always alone,' he responds evasively). Now, Buck is dead, Blanche in a prison hospital, and C.W. (presumably) kept occupied by 'Daddy'. They have shared in a kind of communion of blood: isolated in the incommunicability of pain (hunched in opposite corners of the get-away car) but together in convalescence, and united in the common involvement in bloodshed. But the vital factor, for Clyde, is clearly the decisive establishment of his public identity, through the publication of Bonnie's poem. It is Clyde's realisation that the legend has (as the newspaper editor of Ford's *Liberty Valance* has it) 'become fact', and through Bonnie's poetic gifts, that enables him to make love to her: again, the motivation is partly gratitude, but more than this, a newly-discovered confidence in himself, which the irony (the confidence rests on completely false foundations) makes the more touching. Penn's tenderly ironic treatment of the whole scene is very touching, in fact, with Clyde delighted, not so much by his own or Bonnie's sensual gratification, as by his discovery that he could do it. The shot of the sheets of newspaper blowing away has a characteristically complicated ambiguity: it conveys (supported again by the banjo music) abandonment, freedom, exhilaration; it also suggests a precariousness and fragility that carries multiple overtones, relating to the lovers' relationship, their public identity, their situation.

The same touching immaturity reappears in Clyde's desire to marry Bonnie, to 'make an honest woman of her', now that their relationship has been consummated. Nowhere in Penn's work is the contrast between legend and reality more poignant than in the discrepancy here between ferocious outlaw and hesitant, conventional adolescent. The image evoked of a future normal married life intensifies by contrast the sense of the hopelessness of the position. And when Bonnie yearningly asks Clyde what he'd do if they could begin all over again, his reply is that he'd live in one state and rob banks in others: he is incapable of abandoning his persona, on which his very potency depends. At the same time, the fact that he still needs such an outlet casts further doubt on the depth of his sexual awakening.

Bonnie's poem (reputedly the work of the real-life Bonnie Parker) is a fascinating example of doublethink, or Having It Both Ways. As she first reads it to Clyde they are sitting in their (stolen) white car in the rain: the poem combines an image of the two as desperate and dangerous bandits with a contradictory image of them as essentially pure: 'Honest and upright and *clean*'—an attempt to deny the irremoveability of blood-stains. Hence the complex effect of the film's ending, of which the sense of desecration is only one (though emotionally the dominant) aspect. The stolen white car, the donned white clothes symbolise an artificially assumed, and false, identity, at the same time as they correspond to something the spectator feels to be valid in Bonnie and Clyde. The image of the white bodies spattered with blood (and the slow motion, as well as evoking a sense of ritual, has the effect of hideously prolonging the agony) at last unifies the opposed images of Bonnie and Clyde, hence sums up the ambivalence of the entire film, an ambivalence that has its roots in Penn's tragic sense of existence.

Stills: Bonnie and Clyde.

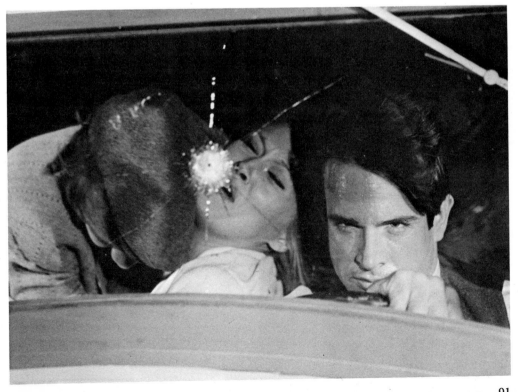

ALICE'S RESTAURANT

'Everyone' – people say to me – 'is making films about hippies now': as if Arthur Penn were being merely fashionable, or trying to 'keep up', or trying to cash in on a popular interest. Which only goes to show how important it is to see an artist's latest work in the context of his whole development. Living (and I mean rather more by the word than just 'existing') in the America of today, and with *The Chase* and *Bonnie and Clyde* behind him, it would be more surprising if Penn *hadn't* made a film about the hippy movement: the logic is perfect and inevitable. Nor is it very surprising that, although plenty of people are going to see the film and Penn is assured of another commercial success and the consequent increase in the possibilities of working in the freedom he would like, explicit reactions have been somewhat lukewarm. This has little to do with the quality of the film and a lot to do with its nature – and with Penn's critical intelligence. *Alice's Restaurant* is unsensational, lacking the startling direct impact of *Bonnie and Clyde*: an essentially gentle film. People who don't like hippies distrust it because it is so sympathetic to hippies; people who *do* like hippies distrust it because it exposes with the most rigorous clarity – the truest sort of clarity, born out of sympathetic insight, not distaste – the essential weaknesses and inadequacies of the hippy movement. Most 'commercial' films about hippies tend to indulge the bourgeois prejudices of their audiences by exploiting the picturesque aspects of the movement, treating hippies as if they were some other animal. Penn gets inside, without ever being *of*, the drop-out community presented in his film. One effect of the resulting complexity of attitude is to make us feel the characters as in essential ways very close to ourselves: we recognise that they are responding to problems of living that confront us all.

There are, of course, hippies and hippies, in the cinema as in real life: Penn's hippies in *Alice's Restaurant*, Godard's hippies in *Weekend*. It is not, I think, primarily a question of true and false – of which director gives us the more realistic picture of hippies, though Penn's are certainly closer to the professed attitudes of the mainstream hippy movement.

In fact (making allowances for the stylised, fable-like nature of Godard's film) both portrayals correspond convincingly enough to things one feels to be going on around one, as does Siegel's again very different version of hippies in *Coogan's Bluff*. One is led to reflect that the word 'hippy' itself has come to cover a great multitude of sins and virtues. The question is rather, why are these directors attracted to such different 'faces' of what is really too diverse to be called a 'movement' (though one doesn't know what else to call it): Godard to militant, murderous hippies who can be readily assimilated into his postulated return to tribal savagery, Penn to a group whose outstanding characteristic is a commitment to passivity? The difference may seem superficially the more surprising in view of Penn's fascination with violence: indeed, he has followed his most violent film with his least violent.

The comparison is given added point by Godard's well-known strictures on *Bonnie and Clyde*. These seem so irrational – so lacking in even the rudiments of critical objectivity – that one looks for some ulterior motive whereby to account for them. One hasn't to look far. Godard has become single-mindedly committed to a belief in the necessity for revolution, and for the attempt to draw up a coherent ideological programme. Bonnie and Clyde are hopeless, inadvertent revolutionaries: they become folk-heroes through a conjunction of circumstances, and never achieve any real awareness of themselves, of the roles they have come to play, or the relation between the two: they muddle through to their horrible and inevitable deaths. Socially, the film could be considered dangerous: it encourages revolt while totally failing (or refusing) to associate revolt with any constructive ideology. Placing Penn's film beside what one might call the 'intention' level of Godard's recent work, it could well seem merely irresponsible. Yet, while Godard's work now seems consciously focused on the defining of an ideology, nothing very coherent or positive has so far emerged: what Jean Pierre Léaud and Juliette Berto discover most convincingly in *Le Gai Savoir* is, in their own words, '*le néant*', and all Godard seems able actually to commit himself to is the hopeful prospect of a return to zero. One respects the rigour of his radicalism: respects the uncompromising renunciation that the decision to make *Le Gai Savoir* represents (respects the decision, however, rather than the actual film). Yet such respect should not prevent one from taking stock of just what Godard has in fact renounced, as artist and human being (I mean of course the human being that is inseparable from the artist – the human personality the films express). The commitment to revolution involves commitment to the principle of the necessity for violence. Godard's films explicitly accept that necessity and at the same time nullify it as a reality: they make violence stylised, painless and often funny. There is no pain in Godard's later films, just as there is no emotion. Human feeling, warm outgoing sympathy, has always been very weak in Godard's work, but lately it has been eradicated altogether – either deliberately, or it has just finally dried up. It becomes rather difficult to see, in human terms, what he conceives revolution as *for*, as human life seems no longer to have much meaning for him.

Penn is at the furthest possible remove from

such abstraction: he is the poet of flesh-and-blood. *Bonnie and Clyde* above all makes violence real, and makes pain real: it does all the things Godard can't do if he is to make his revolutionary commitments acceptable (to himself, perhaps, as well as to his supposed audiences – whatever he now supposes his audiences to be). To put the point at its most crudely physical, it is one thing to make *Weekend*, another to imagine real bullets cutting into real flesh. Godard can't *afford* to like Penn's films. Further, *Bonnie and Clyde*, with

its warmth and generosity towards human beings, is in overall effect tragic and pessimistic. *Weekend* is the work of a fanatical idealist who hates humanity so much as it is that he is forced into the terrible optimism of annihilating civilisation and starting again. (I

Stills: below – after the deconsecration, the keys of the church are handed over to Alice (Pat Quinn) and Ray (James Broderick); right – Officer Obie (William Obanhein) cuts the cake at the opening of Alice's Restaurant.

find it increasingly hard to distinguish Godard's hatred of contemporary western society from a hatred of humanity itself.) Finally, *Bonnie and Clyde* had an exceptional popular success that cut through all class distinctions between workers and bourgeoisie, all race distinctions between black and white. Godard desperately wants to make revolutionary films that will reach 'the people', the workers. If *Le Gai Savoir* – a film during which even seasoned intellectuals leave the cinema or fall asleep – is an example of how

he intends to set about this (it was, after all, made for television), one can see why (all the other differences taken into account) he might bitterly resent Penn's film and its success.

The fundamental difference between Godard and Penn (respectively the most abstract and the most concrete of major directors) can be defined through one example: Penn's use of Officer William Obanheim, the original 'Officer Obie', playing himself in *Alice's Restaurant*. Godard can only allow himself to see the bourgeoisie as a set of two-dimensional

caricatures or an abstraction; to Penn it remains an aggregate of individual human beings. That the character of Obie, one of the film's chief representatives of 'Establishment' respectability, should be presented so affectionately that the real man could be induced to undertake the role, would doubtless seem from a Godardian standpoint evidence of sentimental weakness; to me it is evidence of Penn's refusal to abstract. Abstraction in some form and to some degree, with a consequent hardening of human responses, is the usual concomitant of revolutionary commitments such as Godard's; it becomes that much harder to advocate bloody revolution if one sees its potential victims exemplified in the individual, and likeable, human form of Officer Obie.

In fact, if Godard is still capable of liking any film made within the traditional commer-

Stills: above – Ray; right – Shelly (Michael McClanathan).

cial framework (recent remarks suggest he isn't), that film might well be Peckinpah's *The Wild Bunch*, which seems to offer the following propositions: violence is inherent and ineradicable in human nature (the scorpion-and-ant symbolism, and the children delightedly watching); therefore violence must be accepted; it is better if violence finds some positive (i.e. revolutionary) form of expression, putting itself at the service of some cause (while causes last). This account ignores some of the qualifying ironies of Peckinpah's bitter film, but doesn't I think falsify its overall movement. What one admires (up to a point) is Peckinpah's honesty in refusing to cheat by minimising the effects of violence, or by showing them only on characters whose destruction we can view with satisfaction.

This is not the digression it may appear. *Bonnie and Clyde* and *The Wild Bunch* are two outstanding landmarks in the American cinema's emancipation from taboos on presenting extremes of violence visually, and one learns quite a lot about Penn in comparing them. The most obvious point of comparison (beyond the general one that both films show bandits achieving the status of revolutionaries despite themselves) is the directors' use of slow motion, and it proves very revealing. (One had supposed here the direct influence of Penn's film on Peckinpah's, but this may not be the case: in conversation Penn suggested a common derivation from *The Seven Samurai;* and Peckinpah claims that he used slow motion in certain cut portions of *Major Dundee*, two years before Penn made *Bonnie and Clyde*.) The first rule about slow motion is that it confers a certain beauty on anything to which it is applied, however inherently horrible the image: in slow motion, even violent, clumsy, convulsive actions take on a degree of balletic grace. The effect of slow motion on the deaths of Bonnie and Clyde is very complex. For one thing, our feelings of tenderness and sympathy for the characters are very strong; though we see far more than they see, we feel a close identification with them. Hence we experience the visceral impact of the bullets, and the protracted, lingering feeling of the deaths, with a painfully immediate empathy. Our physical-emotional reaction is intensified by the sense of desecration aroused by the blood-spattered white clothes. This is also, as Penn himself pointed out, the moment when Bonnie and Clyde finally pass

out of reality into myth: the *beauty* conferred by the slow motion – beauty that intensifies rather than nullifies the horror of the scene – gives the deaths a ritualistic quality.

But what is one to make of the far more widespread and apparently indiscriminate use of slow motion in the violent passages of *The Wild Bunch*? I find it very difficult to guess at Peckinpah's intentions from the evidence of the film. He may have been trying to suggest the agonising sense of time stretching out at moments of great stress, suspense or pain (the sort of effect definitively achieved by Hitchcock in the overlapping forward tracks of the horse accident in *Marnie*). Something of this is present in the deaths of Bonnie and Clyde; but it depends above all on our sense of identification with the victims, and we feel no identification whatever with most of the victims of violence in *The Wild Bunch*. And, because we watch the slow motion images there purely objectively, it is the *aesthetic* effect that quickly predominates – the great spurts of blood splashed across the screen in semi-suspension take on a perverse abstract beauty curiously at odds with the apparent aim of presenting the effects of violence with uncompromising realism. One finds oneself asking at what point the acceptance of violence merges into a celebration of violence. And, although there is so much blood in Peckinpah's film, there is surprisingly little sense of pain – the force of which observation will be plainer if one places *The Wild Bunch* beside *Bonnie and Clyde* (for example, the scenes depicting the death of Buck). Penn shows consistently in his films a hypersensitivity to pain, both physical and emotional, and the films encourage a corresponding sensitivity in the spectator;

if *The Wild Bunch* sickens, it also to a considerable degree inures. Penn is too fully and intensely human, both in body and in sensibility, to feel bloody revolution as anything but tragic.

It is perfectly logical, then, that in making a film about drop-outs from contemporary society, Penn should gravitate towards a non-violent group whose password is 'Peace', who are groping towards new religious expression, and whose chief enemy is their own lack of certitude or definition (or ultimately, perhaps, quite simply the fact of death).

Alice's Restaurant seems to me a flawed film, but once one has recognised the flaw it ceases to be very important: being local, it is easy to set aside. The film originated in Arlo Guthrie's recorded song-cum-monologue about garbage disposal and the draft. Besides its humour, and any efficacy it may have as protest (not great, I think: it's too essentially good-natured to arouse strong feeling), the record has its own peculiar charm which the film necessarily obliterates, as it depends on *a*) the perpetually recurring guitar accompaniment and *b*) the monologue's construction, i.e. its existence as a self-contained entity. Guthrie's narrative gives the deceptive impression of rambling inconsequentially, with its incessantly reiterated guitar tune, up to the point where he is asked at the draft interview, 'Kid, have you ever been arrested?', at which moment everything clicks neatly into place and, to point this, the accompaniment pauses for the first time in nearly fifteen minutes: it's a magical moment, for which the film has no equivalent. What one regrets in fact is that the original Guthrie anecdote was retained in the film at all: the film must have outgrown it at quite an early stage. It is ironic that what provided the initial inspiration ends up as an intrusion, interrupting the flow of the film and distracting us from the characters and issues we are most concerned with. Penn recognises the semi-independent nature of this section of the film, seeing it as an 'interlude', distinct from the rest in tone as well as narrative, but I think it is slightly more harmful than he allows:

nearly twenty minutes of screen time is rather much for an 'interlude', and the difference in tone disrupts rather than counterpoints. The episode is often very funny, and some of its best jokes – the eventual disposal of the garbage in New York, the urine gag, the sergeant's

Still: Arlo and Roger (Geoff Outlaw) arrested by Officer Obie.

furtive disappearance behind the door marked 'Secret' – are not in the original monologue as recorded. But the film suddenly descends to an altogether simpler level, its tensions and complexities vanish. The humour itself is much simpler than one is used to in Penn: even the funniest moments in *Bonnie and Clyde* are not free from qualifying emotional tensions. It is slightly disturbing to find Penn willing to present the 'mother-rapers, father-stabbers, father-rapers', etc., on the 'Group W Bench', *à la* Guthrie as all nice fellows really; and with the low angle shot of the sergeant pointing and bellowing, 'Kid, we don't like your kind', the film descends to precisely the sort of comic cliché the record, with its quiet understatement, scrupulously avoids. The note of caricature that runs through the whole sequence is not only absent from the rest of

the film but alien to it. Officer Obie himself changes: the caricature presented in the garbage disposal scenes is a simplification rather than a development of the touchingly bewildered figure, anxious to please yet uneasily aware of being out of his depth, who accepts Alice's coffee during the decorating of the restaurant. To point out that the whole 'monologue' sequence is accompanied by Arlo's narration on the sound-track and can therefore be understood as subjective rather than 'realistic' in presentation helps a bit but not much: it explains the change of tone, but not its function in relation to the rest of the film. Further, I don't think this 'subjective' sequence, though we know it derives from the Arlo of real life, throws much light on the Arlo of the film. People who don't know the record assure me that for them the disruption is less obvious, but I suspect it may also be more insidious: it must be that much harder mentally to detach the 'monologue' sequence from the main body of the film.

For that is what I propose to do, for the remainder of this chapter: taking my cue from Penn himself, who agreed with me that, apart from one or two important details such as Shelly's presence in the court-house, the sequence could be detached and shown independently as a short (one would view it far more favourably as such). The excision made, *Alice's Restaurant* seems to me a perfect work, one of its creator's most assured and most personal successes.

'Remember Alice?' Arlo asks, about a third of the way through the record. In the film we are in no danger of forgetting her: if we had to single out a central figure from its complex pattern of interweaving personalities it would surely be her, with Ray a fairly close second, not because they occupy the most screen-time but because they most engage the spectator's emotions – they, and the triangular relationship of which the drug addict Shelly forms the third side. This aspect of the film offers one of the most moving embodiments of Penn's view of human existence: a half-blind struggle

Stills: opposite – Arlo shows the draft psychiatrist his eagerness to kill; below – Arlo and the father-rapers.

towards self-expression and contact in which creative and destructive impulses intertwine and merge indistinguishably.

The scene in which Shelly and Alice make love offers, both in what it expresses and what it implies, a characteristically vivid and conveniently compact example of Penn's ability to communicate the tangle of moral and psychological tensions he sees as an inescapable condition of human action. He refuses to reduce the significance of the scene to any simple or clear-cut statement; as befits an

artist in the great tradition of the American cinema, he is faithful first to the concrete realities of characters and context, rather than manipulating them to express ideas. *Alice's Restaurant*, the second of Penn's films to be made in complete freedom, suggests that he will never repeat the mistakes of *Mickey One*. As so often with Penn, a crucial factor in the scene – and made beautifully present for the spectator – is vivid physical sensation. When Alice comes to him, Shelly is cleaning a motor-bike with an air-blower, which he turns first on himself, then on Alice. The sexual symbolism is obvious but unstressed: it takes second place to the direct physical effect. One seems to feel the hot night, the cooling air; Alice's thin, transparent garment is blown about her body, revealing its contours and its soft aliveness. But if one's surface reaction is an empathic physical delight, this is troubled by various disturbing undercurrents. Ray is

Stills: below – Shelly, Ray and the hot chili; opposite – Alice's outburst.

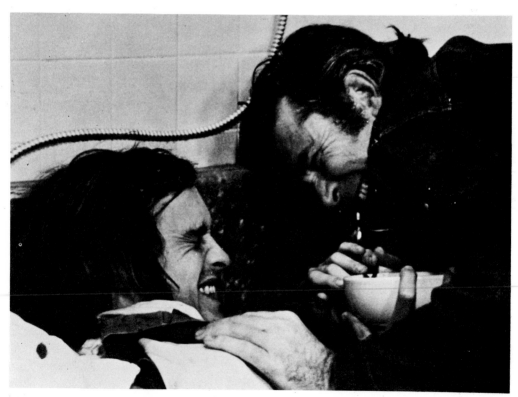

Alice's husband and Shelly's friend. Throughout the film one is aware of a tension between the freedom of the drop-out community – freedom to obey natural impulses as they arise – and the characters' need for stable, dependable relationships: a tension between incompatible 'natural' needs which is fundamental to Penn's view of things, implying as it does important yet irreconcilable drives not merely in this or that society but in the basic conditions of life itself. Ray is kept present in our minds during the scene: it is his motorbike which Shelly is cleaning, and he is cleaning it partly to make up to Ray for beating him in the rally. We remember Ray's pique, intensified when Alice kissed Shelly ('Don't you think he's won enough for one race?'); the association of motor-bikes with virility is again unstressed, but continually felt. We sense the psychological confusions inherent in the three-sided relationship. Alice partly sees herself (and is accepted by others) as a mother-figure: 'Come to mama', she says to Arlo and Roger when she secures their release from jail; and when she runs away from a situation whose tensions have become unbearable, she refers to herself as 'the bitch with too many pups – couldn't take them all milking me'. She is to Shelly both mother and mistress. Similarly, Ray acts as father-figure to Shelly (and to the whole church community), but at the same time one senses latent homosexual feeling between them: it expresses itself most noticeably in their horseplay in the restaurant kitchen, where Ray, forcing over-seasoned food on the younger man, ends up in a 'sexual' position over him, and where one feels that Alice's eruption is provoked by more than the hindrance to her work.

Yet the love-making cannot be seen as only mutual self-indulgence with disturbing (and slightly perverse) overtones. Alice comes to Shelly partly because she is concerned about his drug addiction and wants to help him. He tells her – perhaps rather too emphatically – that he's given it up and will never go back to it; Alice looks sceptical. The love-making develops out of this, and seen in this light reveals further undertones: it is as if Alice were giving herself to him partly as a reward, partly to seal an unspoken contract. It is, up

to a point, a positive and constructive action, fulfilling some of Shelly's immediate needs. Yet it is also, in the long run, unwittingly cruel and irresponsible: the satisfaction is only transitory and partial, and what Shelly needs above all is stability. Alice seems simultaneously to hold out the possibility of this and to withhold it, and the resulting frustration helps precipitate his death.

Such personal issues are given a wider significance by the context which partly determines their nature: the context of the aspirations, part-valid, part-suspect, embodied in the church and its fluctuating community of hippies. I know of no other film that expresses so touchingly the sense of needs left unfulfilled – undefined, even – by the collapse of established religious beliefs and values. This is a theme that runs through Penn's work like a *leitmotiv*. It is there at the outset in *The Left-Handed Gun*: Billy's inability to make contact with the concepts underlying the Easter burning of the straw man or with the tenets of the Bible. It becomes more explicit in *Mickey One* ('Is There Any Word from the Lord?'). It recurs again in Mrs Henderson's enthusiastic but utterly ineffectual prayers in *The Chase*. In *Bonnie and Clyde* it is never raised explicitly, but one is aware throughout of a lack of any directing or controlling sanctions that could give valid purpose to the characters' lives. All Penn's work is concerned with impulses that could be called, in the widest sense, religious: man's blind reaching out towards what lies beyond him, his efforts to break out of the immediate 'reality' which imprisons him: and with the

Still: Ray and Alice at Shelly's funeral.

failure of those impulses to find satisfaction. In *Alice's Restaurant* this theme moves for the first time right to the centre of the film and emerges explicitly as its dominant concern.

Again, the treatment is anything but schematic: a complex pattern of interconnections emerges. On his way to visit his dying father in hospital, Arlo passes a Revivalist meeting in a tent, and pauses to watch the worked-up histrionics of the preacher, which culminate in a very suspect miracle. We feel we are seeing the tail-end of a once rich and fertile popular tradition. The congregation sing a hymn, 'Amazing Grace', a version of which Woody Guthrie used to sing: 'Seems like Woody's road might have run through here sometime,' Arlo comments. The tradition referred to here has two distinguishable branches: folk-song and folk-culture on the one hand (represented in the film by the dying Woody) and orthodox Christianity on the other (the church). Arlo moves repeatedly from Woody to the church community throughout the film, and is ultimately failed by both as far as (in his own words) 'finding out what my thing's going to be' is concerned.

The hospital scenes with Woody are moving by virtue of their intimations of past vitality, present vulnerability. An ageing Pete Seeger sings Woody's songs at his bedside; Arlo arrives and joins in: 'Let's go riding in the car-car'. Woody, mind and senses atrophied by incurable nerve disease, smiles at his son for the first time – his one clear moment of recognition. It testifies to the vitality of the folk tradition to which Woody belonged, but it also leaves one questioning the degree of ultimate satisfaction and sense of meaning (in the face of death) such a tradition can offer.

The values of freedom and alive spontaneity associated with folk art contrast poignantly with the enclosed hospital room and Woody's inertia.

'Amazing Grace' recurs twice in the film: it is sung in the church by the hippy community during the Thanksgiving celebration, and it accompanies the end credits (played on the guitar). It is also referred to once verbally in a line that is one of the keys to the film. Arlo arrives at the church just as the Christian ministers have moved out and Ray and Alice are moving in. Ray declaims histrionically from the pulpit: 'A place to be the way we want to be – at last.' Alice chimes in, 'What more do we want?'. 'Amazing grace', Arlo immediately answers her. But 'amazing grace' never descends, though by the end of the film Arlo and his girl may be moving very tentatively towards it; and the hymn's key line, 'I once was lost but now am found', becomes one of the film's unobtrusive ironies.

Ray fails because he looks for grace in the wrong places: outside himself, instead of within. At the outset of his experiment in living, he tells Arlo that if they'd had the church earlier 'things would have been different' for Roger (Arlo's friend, who has been getting pushed around by the police). Arlo agrees, but looks unconvinced. At the end of the film, with Shelly dead of an overdose in a sordid flophouse, Ray talks of selling the church and buying land to farm. 'We got to have *room*,' he says, then adds, echoing the earlier words about Roger, 'I bet what happened to Shelly never would have happened' if they'd had their 'couple of hundred acres up in Vermont'. He has learnt nothing: he is still projecting his inner failure, his personal insufficiency, on to

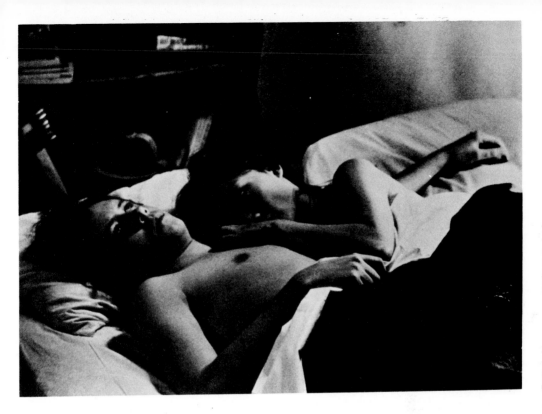

external circumstances. Arlo leaves, with his girl, by way of comment.

But underlying Ray's personal failure is the gap left by the failure of Christianity. The visual beauty of the scene of the church's deconsecration – the evocation of a traditional sense of holiness – is at once intensified and rendered poignant by the desolation, the feeling of things-at-an-end (the congregation is composed almost entirely of old ladies; the use of long-shot emphasises the great empty spaces around them). The church changes hands –

Still: Arlo and Mari-Chan (Tina Chen).

the orthodox ministers give way to seekers after a new 'holiness'. But we gradually realise that they have nothing from which to construct a new religion but the rags and tatters of the old.

The inadequacy of such materials comes across touchingly in the scenes of religious ritual – Thanksgiving, Shelly's funeral, the final 'wedding' – which have a wistful, tentative quality. The Thanksgiving celebrations, in which the ass, Arlo's Thanksgiving present to Ray and Alice with its traditional Christian associations, is a striking visual presence, supply the film's calmest and happiest moments, and suggest the most positive aspects of the 'hippy' aspirations: particularly the sense of a truly multi-racial society forming and living harmoniously, a point the film never has to obtrude because it is simply and beautifully *there*. At the same time, various factors introduce an element of uneasiness. There are the motor-cycles that zoom into the church, nearly killing a baby, reminding us of the undercurrents of violence and aggression existing in *any* community, but likely to be especially strong in one composed largely of drop-outs and misfits (however dedicated to 'Peace'). The communal singing of 'Amazing Grace' is introduced with a montage

Stills: Arlo with Mari-Chan at the 'wedding' (left) and the Thanksgiving present.

of Stockbridge churches, suggesting the possibility of peaceful co-existence within established society through certain shared Christian values; but immediately afterwards comes the garbage disposal sequence culminating in the arrest of Arlo and Roger – peaceful co-exist-

ence proves short-lived. Arlo accompanies the singing of 'Amazing Grace' on the harmonium; near him, side by side, sit Karen, the girl with whom he has been having a brief liaison, and Mari-Chan, the girl in whom he has just begun to show an interest. There is no sign of tension; the girls' proximity suggests, very simply and unobtrusively, how well the moral freedom of the hippies can work, given essentially stable and balanced characters. In close juxtaposition with this, however, we see Ray and Alice making for the belfry (their bedroom) while Shelly watches them with ambiguous jealousy, feeling himself rejected by both and excluded from their relationship. The temporary nature of the gathering is underlined by these suggestions of precariousness. There is also the pervasive threat of conscription, the recurrent reminders of Vietnam, which qualify every move towards stability in the film: the opening draft interview, the negro Jake's metal hook, the suggestion (during the Thanksgiving gathering itself) of escape to Canada. The gift of the ass is a good example of the instability of the values on which the community is based. It is clearly meant to refer to the group's aspirations to 'holiness', yet it is also a joke about holiness: the precise 'tone' of the gift, so to speak, is uncertain. One is reminded of E. M. Forster's comments on the Hindu celebrations in 'A Passage to India': 'By sacrificing good taste, this worship achieved what Christianity has shirked: the inclusion of merriment.' But here the effect is of instability rather than all-inclusiveness. And the ass that looked on at Christ's birth, and on which Christ rode into Jerusalem to be crucified, becomes an animal on which to flee the draft ('I was wondering how I was going to get my ass over the border').

The hippy funeral derives its poignance not only from the snowy setting but from the lack of any real unity: the mourners are scattered haphazardly over the cemetery, no one seems to know quite what to do, the little broken fragments of ritual – the few carnations and chrysanthemums strewn with the falling snow on the coffin, the girl singing – seem more pathetic than meaningful, the centaur painted on the coffin, emblem of harmony between nature and human consciousness, contrasts with the unstable young motorcyclist more than it describes him. The song about 'ageing children' beautifully defines the characters of the film: they have recaptured something of the innocence of children, but find themselves quite unfitted to cope with the questions of meaning and purpose posed by the facts of transience and death.

All these issues come to a head in the 'wedding' of Ray and Alice, where the inadequacies of the hippy movement (as presented) to provide foundations on which secure existences can be built combine with the personal inadequacies of Ray, each illuminating the other. In most respects Ray is a highly characteristic Penn protagonist (though he emerges as rather less sympathetic than his predecessors). He sees himself as a saviour: when he takes over the church, his first action is to place himself against a wall in an attitude of crucifixion, a typically histrionic gesture (and typically accompanied by a self-conscious glance around to make sure his audience – Alice – is appreciating it) expressive of unacknowledged neurotic tensions. A desire for martyrdom, a desire for power: something of the real Ray is revealed in the scene where he finds Shelly's drugs in the 'mobile', beats Shelly, strikes Alice, and, when Arlo tells him to 'cool it', answers him, 'I'm in my church. Where are you?'. It is true that Arlo is nowhere (we see no home, and never think of him as having one); yet, equally, the posses-

Still: Shelly, on drugs again, is brought back to the church by Officer Obie.

siveness and presumption implicit in Ray's remark ('*my* church') strike us as half-pathetic, half-distasteful. Ray may have 'his' church, but it is Arlo who is the more stable personality. Ray embarks on his idealistic venture, in fact, with a fatal lack of self-knowledge or insight into his own motives: essentially, he is another 'blind man battering blind men'. His histrionics conceal him from himself as well as from other people. He is afraid to develop a relationship to any depth of intimacy: he obsessively surrounds himself and Alice with crowds of people, ostensibly from altruistic motives, but really, one feels, to prevent his wife from getting too close to him. Similarly, he enters into a muddled and complex relationship with Shelly which he can't see through to any fulfilment, at once arousing responses in the younger man and cheating them of satisfaction. It is appropriate that Ray's 'Flower Car' becomes Shelly's hearse.

The 'wedding' is notable for the general uncertainty of tone: nobody knows how serious it's meant to be, including Ray and

Stills: Ray at the wedding.

Alice themselves. When Ray suggests it to Alice, he says it's to be 'a real wedding – not like our two-minute special in the court-house. A real church wedding.' In fact, it succeeds in being that only in so far as it takes place in a church. The idea is beautiful: a wedding performed among and by friends as a communal act, in an atmosphere of natural, unconstrained holiness and freedom: but as with all the other celebrations in the film the realisation falls

short of the conception. The ceremony, with a local friend officiating as preacher, is an uneasy parody of the Christian service ('for bad or for better, for drunk or for sober,' etc.) that undermines the traditional sanctities without replacing them with anything new. (Again, comparison with the 'inclusion of merriment' in Forster's Hindu festivities is revealing.) In the ensuing celebrations, Ray sends up balloons, using them as a characteristically histrionic bit of symbolism for ascending to heaven; but heaven merges uneasily into the effects of

113

marijuana ('We're going to get higher and higher'). The party takes on something of the flavour of a Revivalist meeting, with Ray trying to lead a dance and improvise a chant ('It's up there'); but the response is half-hearted. Meanwhile Alice sits in a rocking-chair largely ignored and forgotten, at moments trying to play along, at others looking tired and sceptical. Arlo and Mari-Chan prepare to depart, Ray tries to keep them, suddenly and inconsequentially revealing his idea of selling the church (which a few minutes before he was going to 'reconsecrate'). The underlying sadness and desolation of the whole sequence are crystallised in the shot of the balloons slowly descending over the litter of food and decorations in the now half-deserted church, shown subjectively from Ray's viewpoint as he glances in from the porch. With no stable tradition or set of values from which to draw sustenance, the characters of the film are thrown back on their own inner resources, their weaknesses and inadequacies mercilessly exposed.

The fact of death becomes the crucial test, and is applied particularly to the two young men in the film, Arlo and Shelly. For Arlo it is continually in the background in the form of his dying father and his hereditary nerve disease, which Arlo hasn't got but may develop. Shelly's preoccupation with death, and his attempts to evade its challenge, are suggested more obliquely. Soon after his arrival at the church we see him looking at a memorial tablet embedded in the wall: 'In Loving Memory...'. He hurls a ball at it, as if impotently trying to smash it and what it stands for. It stands in fact for two things: the sense of stable family

relationships as well as a *memento mori*. Another memorial similarly disturbs him later, in the court-house. Shelly dies because life – both his inner life and the life around him – offers him no stability: he can draw no real strength from his messy and uncomfortable relationships with Ray and Alice, and falls back on drugs, both as an escape from the constant awareness of death and a means to the terrible release of death itself. Arlo, on the other hand, moves towards a more courageous and explicit awareness and a more active choice. He tells Mari-Chan that death 'sort of sets you adrift – makes you feel your life is going by. All of a sudden I feel in a hurry to find out what my thing's going to be. Who. And where.' The sequence in which these lines occur comes shortly after the death of Woody, and Mrs Guthrie's words that there will be no funeral – they will take the ashes out to Coney Island and scatter them. The scene opens with a close shot of a flaming, red-hot furnace: we assume we are at Woody's cremation. But it proves to be the furnace of the pottery, in which Mari-Chan is firing her pots. Thus the fact of death is juxtaposed with – even superseded by – the idea of creation. Arlo reveals throughout the film a delicate instinctive moral sense, in his spontaneous yet discriminating responses to the various women who approach him: Renée (the girl with a cold in her nose), Ruth (the middle-aged club owner who talks with a sort of nostalgic disillusionment about 'movements'), Karen, Alice. His *choice* of Mari-Chan (it is the first time we see him taking the initiative in a relationship) emerges out of these progressive discardings. Mari-Chan herself remains something of a cipher, but she is the only character in the film (apart from Arlo

Still: Alice at the wedding.

himself, with his music) whom we see engaged in genuine creative activity – Shelly's mobiles represent attempts at artistic expression whose inadequacy he is half aware of, and a hiding-place for his drugs, the association of the two suggesting the confusion of impulses within him. Arlo's relationship with Mari-Chan is only very tentatively and delicately sketched, but there is sufficient to convey, if no solution to the film's omnipresent and disturbing questions, at least a healthily positive orientation. And their final withdrawal from the church – despite Ray's entreaties – has positive force as comment on Ray and evidence of determination to search further.

But the film ends with Alice, and she is the character with whom the spectator's emotions are most intensely involved. Whatever her relationship to the real Alice Brock, she emerges in the film, through Pat Quinn's remarkable performance, as one of Penn's most fully realised and complex characters, presented with his characteristic combination of sympathetic insight and rigorous clear-sightedness. That extraordinary last shot of the film inevitably evokes comparison with the last shot of Chabrol's *La Femme Infidèle*. The resemblance is purely coincidental, as neither director had seen the other's film at the time of shooting. Both shots are similar (and similarly complex) in technique, combining a simultaneous tracking-out and zooming-in with a lateral movement of the camera; both show a woman left behind. Their function, however, is quite distinct. Chabrol's shot, while not strictly subjective in physical viewpoint, is subjective in effect, expressing the husband's spiritual movement towards his wife as the policemen lead him away from her.

There is no subjective effect in Penn's: Arlo and Mari-Chan have gone, and we have the feeling that their gaze is directed towards the future, not to what has been left behind. Instead, it is *we* who contemplate Alice at such length, during a darkening of the sky that intensifies the scene's unrest and was apparently one of those happy natural accidents that Penn knows how to employ, like the cloud-shadows sweeping over the maize field in *Bonnie and Clyde*. And what we see in Alice, surely, is a reflection of ourselves, of our own confusions and doubts in a world of shifting or disintegrating values.

I don't think *Alice's Restaurant* is, as a friend suggested, the first genuine 'folk' film. Much of the material may have been provided by those actually involved in 'folk' culture (or its present-day extension, the hippy movement), but the film as a whole is decisively dominated by Penn's personality and outlook, its themes are developments of the themes of his earlier films, the characters and the way they are treated are in direct line of descent from their predecessors. And that outlook has only very limited affinities with 'folk' art and the hippy movement, although it is intensely sympathetic to both. Penn's love of the spontaneous and impulsive – of the whole side of us that is rooted in our physical-instinctual being – is balanced by a movement towards full awareness and conscious evaluation that sets him apart from his characters (though he never for a moment condescends to them). Folk art, the hippy community, Arlo Guthrie, are the *material* of *Alice's Restaurant;* it is (with the exception of the section derived from the recorded monologue) very much Arthur Penn's film.

SHOOTING ⬛
LITTLE BIG MAN

Arthur Penn's seventh film, due for release in the winter of 1970, is *Little Big Man*, from a novel by Thomas Berger. The screenplay is by Calder Willingham, the cameraman is Harry Stradling Jr, and the stars are Dustin Hoffman, Faye Dunaway, Richard Boone and Martin Balsam. The film is in Panavision, a big production financed by CBS, and will probably run for about 2 hours, 40 minutes – Penn's longest and most expensive film to date. Shooting was completed in Winter 1969, and at the time of writing, Penn and the indispensable Dede Allen are 'extracting' the film from 'the basic raw material' (his own description of the editing process).

Berger's novel is about a white boy called Jack Crabb (Hoffman) brought up for five years by the Cheyenne (with whom he earns the name Little Big Man), then shuttled by circumstances back and forth between the Cheyenne and the whites. Crabb, who claims to be the only white survivor of Custer's last stand at the Little Big Horn, tells the story himself in rambling reminiscence, at the age of 111 (in the film this is updated to 121). His narrative forms a picaresque, freely episodic novel of over 400 pages, characterised by a brutal and ironic humour, encompassing most of the half-historic, half-legendary figures of the West – Custer, Wyatt Earp, Kit Carson, Wild Bill Hickok, Calamity Jane, Buffalo Bill – as well as numerous fictitious characters, both Indian and white. In the course of the narrative, Crabb acquires two wives, one white (a Swedish girl called Olga), one Cheyenne (Sunshine). The book's most interesting achievement is, through Crabb's alternation between the white and Indian worlds, the development within a single consciousness of a dual outlook – white world seen through Indian eyes, Indian through white. This may be difficult to realise in cinematic terms, perhaps, though both Penn and his producer, Stuart Millar, hope something of it will emerge.

Calder Willingham's script seems admirable *qua* screenplay: spare and skeletal, providing a firm structure and strong dialogue, but with

Photograph: Indian villagers.

118

no pretensions to self-sufficiency, leaving the essential creation of each scene to the director. It is a remarkable feat of compression and re-organisation. Of the semi-historic figures, all but Custer and Hickok have been eliminated; elsewhere, while the alternating rhythm of the narrative has been retained, its structure has been tightened by the telescoping of certain characters, so that in the film an earlier character recurs where in the novel an entirely new one appears. For example, in place of Crabb's niece Amelia, whom he rescues from a brothel in the last third of the novel, the film brings back Mrs Pendrake (Faye Dunaway), Crabb's white 'mother' by adoption who very quickly reveals erotic designs on him. This substitution, which apparently has Berger's enthusiastic assent, provides a very logical development for the Mrs Pendrake of the earlier scenes. Faye Dunaway's part, nonetheless, remains relatively small: it is Little Big Man's film, and Hoffman appears in every scene.

Another change, while less immediately striking, seems even more important. In Berger's novel, Little Big Man remains to the end an essentially passive figure: even when he is jolted into deliberate activity, as he is by the abduction of his Swedish wife by Indians, he fails to sustain his purpose. In the script, he gradually develops a strong emotional commitment to the Indian cause, and by the end is a far more conscious and positive figure than he ever becomes in the book, although, this being a Penn film, he affects the outcome of events only in a confused and ironic way. The change first becomes noticeable in the protagonist's attitude to buffalo hunting: in the book he joins in the slaughter of buffalo for hides quite without conscience; in the script

he is invited and refuses, acknowledging the dependence of the Indians on the buffalo herds for meat. The script builds to a passionate protest at what was done to the Indians. One might criticise this for making explicit what in the novel is expressed very obliquely, through irony. Yet I think it will emerge logically from the film. Where the script can be faulted is in the partial softening of the Cheyenne character, though more by omission than by actual distortion. It is greatly to Berger's credit that he gains our sympathy for the Indians without sparing us any of the aspects of their behaviour that are likely to appal the white sensibility: after battles, for example, the Cheyenne women – gentle and tender wives and mothers, perhaps, in their daily lives – go out with knives to mutilate the bodies of the dead soldiers. Such details have scant representation in the script. A 'romantic' idealisation of the Indians is a perfectly logical corollary of the social attitudes of *The Chase* and *Bonnie and Clyde*, but the validity of any idealisation is weakened by a reluctance to face the harsher and more disquieting realities of whatever is being idealised.

The film has been shot in Hollywood, and on location in Montana and Alberta. At Penn's invitation I spent four days at Calgary, watching the shooting. The location was forty miles from Calgary, at the foot of the first foothills of the Rockies, where about fifty tepees had been erected within the bend of a river. The team had come to film scenes of life in an Indian village, culminating in the massacre of the Washita river, when Custer slaughtered an entire Cheyenne community – men, women, children, and even the ponies. But Penn had come to Canada for snow, and when I arrived there was no sign of it: green grass, bright sunshine, sparkling water, the Rockies clearly visible in the distance, and everyone anxiously glancing around for signs of heavy cloud. So Penn was shooting one of the last scenes of the film, where Old Lodge Skins, Jack Crabb's Cheyenne 'father', played by a 70-year-old Indian chief, prepares to die. He emerges, blind and aged, from the tepee, and asks Jack, who is lame from wounds received at the Little Big Horn, to lead him up the mountain. He feels that not only his own life, but the way of life of his people, the 'Human Beings' (the Cheyennes' name for themselves), and even the race itself, are nearing their ends. 'Oh, it will take them time, but the whites will rub out the Human Beings, my son . . . This was a perfect place until the white men came. Buffalo and game were everywhere. The grass was green, the water sweet, and the sky blue.' It was the ideal introduction to the film, a moment of extraordinary Pirandellian intensity, the lines spoken by the old Indian, acting blind, against a background of grass as green as one could wish, and under a sky as blue, to cameras trained on him by white Americans, under a white American's direction.

Snow fell dutifully all that night, and next morning the location was transformed. All bright colours had disappeared. Under a thick grey sky from which snow continued to fall heavily, the river flowed darkly through a white world against which stood the dun tepees capped with snow, and black firs. Dean Tavoularis, art director on *Little Big Man* (and previously on *Bonnie and Clyde*) told me: 'Indian things can look very circusy and kind of Halloweenish. We tried to mute all the colours down, and marry them to the ground.'

I watched Penn shoot several tracking and panoramic shots through the village, with quite complex interweaving actions – Indians engaged in various activities – in foreground, middle distance and long-shot. One panning-shot, for example, has young Indians fishing in the river in distant long-shot; an Indian on a horse starts up the bank, winds through the village in medium long-shot, moving out of and later back into the image; smoke issues

Photograph: Penn on location.

from the vents of tepees; children play and chase each other in the snow; a horse drags a load of firewood on wooden runners; the camera picks up the horseman again as he rides off to the right. The extras (all North American Indians) are wrapped in blankets coloured with what look like natural dyes: dull maroon, dirty pink, steely blue – the only colours other than greys, blacks, browns. The subdued colouring, and the sense of constant movement in the environment – the carefully organised details of Indian life – should give the snow scenes a restrained visual poetry.

Arthur Penn is as far removed as possible from the stereotyped image of the movie director: the loud-mouthed dictator glued immovably to the director's chair and bellowing orders through a megaphone. It would probably take an unprepared onlooker some time to decide, on the set of *Little Big Man*, who *was* the director. But, although he is so quiet and unobtrusive (I heard him raise his voice perhaps twice or three times in four days, to call for silence), one soon realises that Penn is omnipresent. There were times when he would be standing beside me, then, when I turned, he had disappeared, and I would at last make him out again in some distant part of the set re-arranging a detail with a technician or an actor. Penn doesn't dominate, he pervades: discussing and rehearsing with the actors, checking the image through the viewfinder, re-arranging details of make-up, dress, props, discussing with his assistant director points of background movement involving untrained extras, not above lending a hand to help move a tepee a few feet. Above all, one

Photograph: Amy Eccles as Sunshine.

sees him *listening*, and comes more fully to appreciate the collaborative nature of his art. He will listen to suggestions from anyone, but especially from his actors. Yet equally one senses that the real decisions are always Penn's, that he makes the suggestions of others his own by adopting them and assimilating them into his own sense of how the shot in question should go.

Penn gets such marvellously alive performances from his actors because he respects them. There is likely to be a close relationship between a director's treatment of his actors and his attitude to the characters the actors are creating. Thus von Sternberg's vaunted total control over his players' every gesture and expression is closely related to the sense of fatality in his films. The quality of Penn's characters, even very minor ones (there are about ten good examples in *Alice's Restaurant* alone), as people living and responding spontaneously, links with his love of spontaneous contributions from his actors, his fondness for encouraging the unrehearsed response. Dean Tavoularis had come to *Little Big Man* straight from *Zabriskie Point*. Understandably, as an art director he had found working for Antonioni more fulfilling: he was given much more to do. But he spoke of Penn with great respect, and expressed the essential difference between the two directors' approaches rather well: 'Arthur is very intent on getting that moment of truth between two actors going through a scene. It is very interesting to watch him work, as he goes over and over the scene until it happens.' For Antonioni, on the other hand, the art director is probably a more important collaborator than the actors: he 'treats his actors as part of the visual whole –

there is none of the search that Arthur goes through to get this thing going between actors.' Penn likes working with intelligent actors who want to contribute actively to the film, and they like working with him. He spoke of Marlon Brando, for instance, with the greatest warmth and enthusiasm. Brando has a reputation for being 'difficult' with directors, but clearly there was no difficulty during the filming of *The Chase* (with one rather extraordinary exception: Brando didn't want Calder to beat the killer of Bubber Reeves – the moment to which the whole film moves). But actors like Brando and Dustin Hoffman are more intelligent and sensitive, have greater artistic integrity, than some of the directors they work for. If Hoffman protested, during the filming of *The Graduate*, that Mike Nichols was sacrificing motivation and human reality for the sake of 'cute' and shallow effects, can anyone deny that Nichols's victory in the finished film proves the protest fully justified?

In *Little Big Man*, Penn is working within the 'classical' Hollywood tradition from a script not his own: an admirable opportunity to observe the contribution a director can make during shooting. I watched Penn work on the scene in which Little Big Man's Indian wife Sunshine introduces her three sisters, all widowed by the whites, with a view to getting her husband to accept them as extra wives. In the script, the scene runs as follows:

EXTERIOR – JACK'S TEPEE
SUNSHINE AND JACK – DAY

Sunshine stops preparing food, moves aside the bowl, sits beside Jack and starts scraping a buffalo robe.

SUNSHINE (*feels of her swollen belly*):Your new son is kicking very hard today. I think he wants to come out and see his father.
JACK: Tell him to wait till I finish my dinner.
SUNSHINE: I'll tell him, but I don't think he'll wait much longer. (*speaks to baby, gravely*) Stay in there, don't come out till your father eats. (*a bit slyly*) It's a good thing I have a strong brave husband who brings in so much game and food.
JACK (*happily*): Mmmm-hmmm . . .
SUNSHINE: My strong husband brings in much more than we need.
JACK (*sleepily*): Ummm-mmm, be quiet, woman. I'm meditating.
SUNSHINE (*silent for a moment, but obviously has something important to say*): There are many Human Beings here, many bands from many places. But it's sad . . . many husbands have been rubbed out by the white man.
JACK (*with mild annoyance*): The rattle of your tongue disturbs me, woman.
SUNSHINE: It's sad because many women sleep alone and cry.
JACK (*not really unkind, calm and matter-of-fact*): Be silent now, or I'll beat you.
SUNSHINE (*pauses*): Yes, but I think my sisters are here.
JACK (*opens his eyes*): Your *what*?
SUNSHINE (*meekly*): My sisters. Digging Bear, Little Elk and Corn Woman. I think they are here.
JACK: What do you mean, you *think* they are here?!
SUNSHINE (*very meekly*): I believe they are. You bring much more food than we need.

Photograph: Jack – Little Big Man (Dustin Hoffman) and Sunshine.

(*Jack stares in consternation and Sunshine bows her head, sniffling*) It is very sad. They have no husband, and they cry.

JACK: That's too bad! . . . I'm sorry.

SUNSHINE: Digging Bear had a baby and lost it, and so did Corn Woman. Poor Little Elk never had any baby at all.

JACK: All right, what do you want *me* to do about it?

SUNSHINE (*smiles*): I knew you would understand.

There is no breakdown of this dialogue into close-ups, two-shots, etc., no indication of camera positions or angles. Penn shot it intact a large number of times using about four different set-ups (and different lenses), so that the scene was covered in medium two-shot

Photographs: left – Hoffman; above – Penn.

from different angles, in close-up of Hoffman, and in close-up on Amy Eccles (the Chinese girl who plays Sunshine). Altogether, the actors played through the scene at least a dozen times, not counting rehearsals. This shooting method – not uncommon in essentials, but carried to extremes by Penn – has advantages from various viewpoints. It enables the actors to develop their own performances, discovering new possibilities of expression and

embellishment; when new or inexperienced players are involved (there are many in *Little Big Man*), repetition before the cameras is much the best way to help them gain the confidence necessary to build their characterisations. There is the accompanying danger of boredom for the experienced performer; but as Penn suggested to me, even boredom can at times goad actors into sudden new spontaneous impulses. The length of the take enables the players to feel the continuity of the scene, without having their performances fragmented more than necessary into pre-determined close-ups, medium shots, etc. For Penn and Dede Allen, when they edit the film, the method provides an enormous range of choice: even failed-takes may provide expressive fragments that can be used. One begins to appreciate how the richness and concentrated density of effect in so many scenes in Penn's films are achieved. This whole shooting and editing method relates very interestingly to Penn's themes and attitudes, the view of life his films express. The behaviour of his protagonists is always instinctive and empirical, at worst a blind muddling through, at best (Annie Sullivan) a creative groping after expression and control. They are always too involved in the struggle of existence to dominate and order it externally; instead, they pursue their inner drives towards what they want, hardly knowing in advance what it is. The chief difference between their efforts and Penn's is that his are usually successful.

Only minimal alterations were made to Calder Willingham's dialogue as the scene between Jack and Sunshine evolved, for example Hoffman repeating the sisters' names in comic incredulity. The only major change to the script was Penn's decision to shoot the scene in the snow. There was much discussion on the location about the probability of Indians cooking and eating *outside* the tepee with snow actually falling. I think that the licence, if it is one, will be justified by the results: it will intensify the sense of Jack's Indian-ness at this stage in his life, his adaption to a hard and stoical existence. The scene's surface comedy will be counterpointed by the setting of desolate snowy wastes. Penn introduced some background detail into the scene – a depleted Indian family gathering at their cooking-fire in long-shot, stoic old man and children – which should heighten this effect. In the course of shooting, small touches began to accumulate of the kind that, apparently insignificant individually, lend a scene character and particularity. Instead of having Sunshine merely prepare the dinner, Penn had her serve it and Jack eat it: 'Be quiet, woman, I'm meditating' became the more prosaic and practical 'Be quiet, woman, I'm digesting'. Characteristically, Penn had rejected authentic Indian spoons in favour of the more directly physical effect of fingers dipped in hot gravy. As take followed take, the 'buffalo stew' became hotter and hotter over the fire; at last Hoffman resorted to the expedient of dropping lumps of snow into his food to cool it. Finally, Penn had Amy Eccles scrape the left-over scraps back into the cooking-pot with her fingers. And so the scene began to take on a highly characteristic physical immediacy together with its complex tone of humour and uneasy melancholy.

Yet Penn feels very intensely the limitations of working within the classic Hollywood tradition, even to the point where he denies the possibility of his making *Little Big Man* a truly personal film. Watching the shooting at Calgary makes it easy for me to understand his position, without necessarily agreeing with it. The point is the more worth making in that, in this instance, there is no question of the usual tensions – domination by the producer, studio interference – one thinks of as jeopardising the work of Hollywood directors. The producer, Stuart Millar, a man of charm and

Photograph: Penn, holding the authentic Indian spoons, with Amy Eccles.

129

intelligence, is a personal friend of Penn's and obviously trusts him absolutely. Millar, who has been personally involved in the project from a very early stage, visits the set daily, taking the keenest interest in the shooting, metaphorically (and unobtrusively) patting people on the back, but never interfering. Two things chiefly worry Penn – in conversation he reverts to them repeatedly: the great weight of machinery, both literal and metaphorical, involved in a big production, and – curious as it may at first seem – the sheer professionalism of the technicians, experts who have their own highly developed but orthodox and 'anonymous' ways of doing things, and resent being asked to do them differently. Anything personal and unorthodox Penn wished to do would have to be enforced against a great deal of opposition, perhaps one-part spoken to four-parts silent. One realises why only a certain kind of sensibility can flourish in the traditional Hollywood set-up: a sensibility, first, that can express itself adequately in traditional forms and by traditional means (the sort of professionalism Penn finds an obstruction obviously suits Hawks, for example, perfectly) and, second, that is itself insulated within a certain professional toughness. I wouldn't dream of describing Ford, Hitchcock and Hawks as insensitive; but neither would I use the word 'sensitivity' of them in quite the way I would use it of Penn. For a man of his sensitivity, it is the intangibles that really count: the sense of being surrounded by a great pressure of wills not necessarily hostile, but with a purely professional rather than creative interest in their work. I asked Harry Stradling how he liked

Photographs: star and extras.

130

working for Penn. He said he liked it fine – Penn doesn't ask for many tracking shots. Stradling is one of Hollywood's great professional cameramen – Penn himself spoke of him with respect – but for him, and for the rest of the crew of over a hundred and fifty *Little Big Man* is clearly just another job, to be executed with the greatest possible efficiency and the minimum of personal engagement.

The film will not, then, emerge as the direct personal statement Penn would like to be making. Yet it seems to me that it may well be a more personal work than he realises, involved as he is in executing another man's script and frustrated by the sense of the limitations and obstacles in the way of direct personal expression. When one considers the various stages in the creation of the film, Penn is seen to be the one constant factor. Choice of subject: Berger's novel may not have been an entirely free choice in the way in which the subjects of *Mickey One* and *Alice's Restaurant* were, but neither was it in any sense imposed on Penn, and he has long been interested in the project of making a film about the Indians and their fate. Beyond this, the novel's central figure reveals certain clear affinities with Penn's protagonists. Near the end of the book Jack says to Old Lodge Skins (the lines are not used in the screen-play): 'Grandfather, few people have your great wisdom. The rest of us are often caught in situations where all we can do is survive, let alone understand them. So with me, Little Big Man.' If Billy Bonney had been more articulate, he could have said the same to Mr Tunstall, and (with a similar proviso) the words might have been echoed by Mickey, by Bubber Reeves, by Bonnie and Clyde, by Alice, Ray and Shelly. Preparation of the script: Penn made it clear that the screenplay is Calder Willingham's own – he contributed less of the dialogue than usual in his films. Yet the script grew out of consultations between Willingham and Penn over a period of years. Shooting: Penn, whatever restrictions on his freedom he may feel, demonstrated to me very convincingly that his influence is all-pervading. Editing: Penn is resuming his 'frequently heated, but always loving' dialogue with Dede Allen. There is more than one kind of *auteur* film.

The rushes of *Little Big Man* looked very promising, and often very Penn-like in their aliveness; some of the long takes were so beautiful that I found myself regretting that they would probably be fragmented in the editing, until I began to sense, as take followed take on the screen, the impact, richness and complexity that selection and cutting would give. The seemingly simple choice between alternative takes from an identical set-up must often present great problems. I saw the rushes of a scene where Jack and his Swedish wife Olga (another promising newcomer, Kelly Jean Peters) watch the contents of their home being sold by public auction, Olga crying hysterically. In one early take, and only one, the wind blew Olga's hair across her face, giving her a more vulnerable look; in other respects the take was inferior to later ones. What considerations guide a director's choice? I was struck even more by the possibilities editing offers for controlling and changing the emotional emphasis of a given scene, for increasing or diminishing its complexity. In medium shot, Olga seemed predominantly a comic creation, her hysterics verging on caricature; in close-up, huddled against

Jack's chest, though there was no detectable change in the actual performance, she seemed genuinely pathetic and lost.

On the strength of what I saw I look forward to *Little Big Man* with high expectations. If the film has a deficiency, I think it may be in the realisation of the Indian characters. If so, it will be a case of an honourable near-miss rather than a disaster. Great care has been taken over the details of Indian life: Penn seemed to me to be catching beautifully all its exterior features, its physicality, its hardness, and to be successfully avoiding the merely picturesque. It was pleasing to discover that certain characters and details from the novel that necessarily seem odd or alien have been retained, notably the 'Contrary', Younger Bear, a Cheyenne who has elected to do everything backwards except fighting. I saw the rushes of a scene where, going to bathe, he 'washes' himself in dust then 'dries' himself in the river. Some of the older Indian extras were able to remember 'Contraries' from their childhood. There is also the *heemaneh*, or homosexual Indian, Little Horse, who dresses as a woman and is accorded an honourable place in Cheyenne society. In most Hollywood adaptations, these would have been the first characters to be eliminated. Then again, careful thought has been given to casting the Indian parts: Old Lodge Skins, his wife, Little Horse, two of Sunshine's sisters, are all played by real Indians. Where it proved impossible to find an Indian suitable for a part, Penn and Millar took a hint from the end of Berger's novel, where the aged Little Big Man, in an old folks' home, complains of television westerns in which Indians are played by Italians or Russians, and adds: 'If the show people are fresh out of real Indians, they should hire Orientals to play them parts; for there is a mighty resemblance between them two, being ancient cousins. Look at them without bias and you'll see what I mean.' Yet for an artist, care and thought are no substitute for intuitive insight: however much research he does, however much detail he works out, there is still the problem of 'realising' characters who are the products of a culture not his own, who think and feel with subtle differences. Necessarily, the Cheyenne characters speak English; but for a director as physical as Penn, the way a character speaks is inseparable from the way he moves, the gestures he makes, from all that sense of inner life Penn's characters communicate. The problem begins as a verbal one and quickly becomes much more. I watched the rushes of a scene near the end of the film where Younger Bear (a spirited and intense Latin-American actor called Cal Bellini), whose life Jack once saved, tells Jack, after rescuing him from the Little Bighorn massacre, that they are even at last, and next time they meet 'I can kill you without becoming an evil person'. There were many takes, and the divergence between them was noticeably greater than in any of the other rushes I saw, as if Penn and Bellini were trying out every possible delivery of the lines in a somewhat desperate attempt to find the right one. We can be confident that Penn won't give us stereotyped Hollywood 'redskins'; it remains to be seen whether his Indian characters will achieve quite the living particularity we have come to expect in his films.

Photograph: Hoffman and Amy Eccles (seated on ground) talk to Penn during shooting.

PROBLEMS OF EDITING

The Elizabethan – Jacobean drama presents innumerable problems of authorship, ranging from the minuscule to the enormous. The possibilities of collaboration, revision by other writers, excisions from and additions to the texts by producers, actors, etc., are responsible for many critical and scholarly headaches and temptations (it becomes so easy to attribute to Shakespeare all the lines you admire and discover 'internal evidence' for attributing those you dislike to other hands). Who really wrote the suspect 'witch' scenes in 'Macbeth'? Why is the play so short? Who wrote the Jupiter scene in 'Cymbeline'? Is 'Titus Andronicus' really Shakespeare's? How much of 'Henry VIII' is by John Fletcher? It may be easy to guess that Shakespeare took over 'Pericles' at the beginning of Act III; but did he write all that comes after and none before? What *kind* of collaboration was the play the result of? It would presumably not have been very difficult to find these things out at the time. No one bothered, because no one took Shakespeare seriously enough.

Multiply these problems by several hundred, and you will have some idea of the problems that are going to confront scholars and critics of the American cinema in the coming centuries. The concept of the American cinema engaging scholars and critics in the kind of way the Elizabethan drama has for the past three hundred years will doubtless still seem merely amusing to many people, including, ironically enough, many of those Shakespearian academics who are wrestling with precisely the sort of problems I have in mind. But it sounds much less silly now than it did a mere ten years ago, and no one who is really aware of the way things are going can doubt that by the end of the present century the study of Hollywood films will have become academically respectable, and from an artistic, not merely sociological, viewpoint. In some ways one's heart quails at this, the scholars having done so much to turn Shakespeare – the most alive and passionate writer of all time – into a stuffed museum piece ('Did their Catullus walk that way?'). One has nightmare visions of the issuing of annotated editions of *Bringing up Baby*. But whether we like it or

134

not it's going to happen, and it will at least mark the acceptance of the Hollywood cinema into the mainstream of western culture and the development of the arts, where it belongs, along with. Renaissance painting, Elizabethan drama, the Viennese symphony, the Victorian novel . . . What is needed, and urgently, is a work of the most rigorous and detailed research into what happens to individual films by important directors: who exactly did what, what degree of control the director had over a) the script, b) the shooting, c) the editing, what cuts were made, and at what stage (editing, censorship, distribution), what things the director was prevented from doing, what scenes were shot by other directors or by assistants. The difficulties of such an undertaking would be daunting, in many cases already insuperable (one cannot imagine that our hypothetical researcher would always get the degree of co-operation he would ideally require). Meanwhile, occasional critics like myself can make minor contributions whenever any reliable information comes their way.

Penn attaches great importance to the editing of his films. The work on the set with actors and camera crew, though 'sometimes passionate and very rewarding', is for him 'the making of a kind of basic raw material from which one will eventually extract a film'. In view of this, it is obvious that *The Left-Handed Gun* and *The Chase*, the editing of both of which was taken out of Penn's hands entirely, pose particular problems for the critic. Ultimately, I think, we can only attempt to evaluate the films as we have them, rather than the hypothetical works Penn himself might have 'extracted' from the 'raw material' he had made, and in discussing these two films I have taken what may seem the easy, but is also in practical terms the only possible, way out. There can be no doubt, however, that both films would have been appreciably different if Penn had retained control of them to the end, and little doubt that they would have been appreciably better.

Penn seems on the whole less upset over the fate of *The Left-Handed Gun* than over that of *The Chase*, although the treatment accorded it would appear even more drastic: at least everything in *The Chase* was shot by him. His first cut of *The Left-Handed Gun* ran for three hours, forty minutes (he admits to inexperience, on his first film). He intended that a great deal of this length should be removed. but isn't at all happy about the final editing. Some scenes move more slowly and laboriously than he intended: he agrees with me, for example, that the scene of Celsa's seduction is somewhat turgid as it stands. The crude 'flames of passion' symbolism of the blazing straw man (see page 27) is not his: he had a long take of the straw figure blazing and burning down, and intended to use only the *end* of this (the editors used the beginning). On the other hand, a lot of what Penn describes as 'remarkable footage' of spontaneous play between the young men was jettisoned. There is still quite a bit of this in the film (in the bathtub scene where Billy plans the initial revenge, the flour fight, and when the gang arrive for Pat's wedding), but apparently it was meant to recur much more and to lighten the tone considerably. Penn conceived the whole film as – although perhaps rather longer than it stands – faster moving and lighter in 'feel' (more, one guesses, like *Bonnie and Clyde*). The ending of the film (Mrs Garrett appearing from nowhere to lead Pat home after Billy's death) wasn't shot by Penn. The ending he *did* shoot, and likes, shows Mexican women with candles gathering around Billy's body, preparing to carry it in procession through the streets. Finally, Penn had no control over the music, and (rightly, I think, for the most part) detests it: there is a particularly clumsy and absurd moment in the scene where Billy returns to the abandoned hut after his escape from jail and finds the dead Charlie's home-made flute. The music wells up on the sound-track as he raises the flute to his lips, pauses abruptly for him to blow three notes, then surges in again. The only music Penn wanted anywhere in the film (apart from the mechanical music-player in the hotel) was Charlie's flute. He equally detests the ballad that accompanies the credits, not for what it says, but on the grounds that since *High Noon* the accompanying ballad had become the sort of cliché he wanted to avoid.

There are two main objections to the editing of *The Chase*, one general, one local. The general one is that again and again throughout the film the take selected by the editors is not the one Penn would have chosen. Usually, he told me, it was the more conventional take that was retained, in preference to the more spontaneous and exciting one; especially, he regrets the loss of various takes in which Brando improvised around 'stilted and excessively expository' passages in the text.

The local objection is to cuts, which can be pinned down with some exactitude. There are a number of scenes or parts of scenes detailed in the final shooting script which Penn says he shot but which are absent from all prints of the film I have been able to see. *When* they disappeared is uncertain: some were doubtless removed by the editors (working under in-structions from Sam Spiegel); others may be distributors' cuts, to reduce the film's length, and some of these may have been made only in the British copies (though a print I saw in Finland was identical with those shown in Britain). Whatever the explanation, I have never seen, in about eight viewings of the film, the following passages (in chronological order as they occur in the script):

1) Between the scene of the spreading of the news of Bubber's escape, and the introduction of Jake, a scene in Briggs's real estate office. Briggs tells a negro called Sam that he is 'respectful to coloured people', but goes on to raise the interest on Sam's overdue mortgage payments. As the film stands, we only glimpse Briggs's office and scarcely have time to associate him with real estate. The scene defines his character clearly, and takes up the theme of the status of negroes, which should run through the film as a recurrent motif.

2) Between the introduction of Jake and the introduction of Anna, a scene in the 'barracks area' where the Mexicans employed by Val Rogers live. Jake stops there on his way to Anna from the (potential) oil-field. The workers complain that they haven't been given a raise in salary; the sycophantic foreman calls them ungrateful – Mr Rogers has installed a television for them. The foreman's wife shows Jake pictures of his wife Elizabeth which she has cut out of the society section of a magazine. The scene adds further detail to the social structure, tells us something important about Val *before* he appears, and establishes Jake's ironic yet impotent attitude to his father, and his equally ironic attitude to his wife.

3) At the end of the scene where Calder tells Mrs Reeves of Bubber's escape, a continuation

inside the house where the Reeves discuss the escape and Mrs Reeves wonders where she 'went wrong' in bringing Bubber up.

4) Between Calder's visit to Sol's cafe and Bubber's climb into the refrigeration truck on the train, a scene on a bus showing Anna on her way to the motel for her rendezvous with Jake. A man advises Anna to put the package she is carrying on the seat beside her, to keep a negro woman off. Anna at once makes room for the woman. The man gets an attractive white girl, who got on the bus at the same stop as the negress, to sit by him, making a remark about 'keeping his suitcase handy'. The girl calls across to the negress, addressing her as 'Mama', they find a seat together, and the man goes to sit beside Anna (who puts her package in the way, but he removes it). He then tries to interest Anna in 'buying a pretty girl like you a drink'. Anna encouragingly says she'll tell him a secret: 'My mammy was a nigger, my pappy was a spick, and they were both Jews. My grandma never married because she was a Chink. And I'm not sure that I'm over a bad case of the measles.' Besides continuing the 'colour' motif, this scene decisively establishes Anna's character at the outset: as the film stands, the spectator only gradually comes to realise how he is to take her.

5) Between the brief sequence of Edwin waiting in his car near the jail and the scene where Ruby shows Calder her new dress (Val's present to her), a short exchange on the jailhouse steps between Cutie (one of the teenagers) and Slim (Calder's deputy). Cutie mentions the teenagers' party arranged for that evening, and (humorously) asks for protection from Bubber.

6) Various small bits for minor characters at Val's party, rather caricaturish.

7) Elizabeth watching Jake's departure from the party; she gets into her car and drives off.

8) A dialogue between Mr and Mrs Briggs before they reach the Reeves's house on their evening walk. They see a poster advertising a nude show. Mrs Briggs: 'You know, Billy, I don't think I ever saw a naked woman.' Briggs: 'I never have, either.' Then they see the gentlemen from the Dentists' Association outing emerging rowdily from the hotel. Mrs Briggs: 'What do you think they had for dinner?' Briggs: 'Dirty jokes.' Mrs Briggs: 'I never heard a dirty joke.' Briggs: 'I never have, either.'

9) After the meeting between Bubber and Lester, a sequence at the Stewarts' party. The guests watch a television news report – pictures of the body of the man Bubber's fellow-fugitive killed. Then a scream from the next door bushes: Cutie thinks she's seen Bubber. It turns out to be a young negro, Roy (who doesn't appear at all in the prints I've seen). The male guests catch him, he says indignantly, 'You got a private street with a white sidewalk?'. Archie (Bubber's eventual killer, who never speaks in the film) takes him by the lapels and nods slowly. Calder arrives in time to break things up.

10) After Jake's and Anna's fruitless search at the broken-down summer-house, a scene where Mrs Henderson (the half-crazy old religious lady) comes to tell the Reeves about the murder, and prays. Mr and Mrs Reeves go upstairs and get things out to sell: Mrs Reeves mentions selling the house, Mr Reeves protests, then gives in. Meanwhile, Mrs Henderson wanders around below, singing hymns.

11) During the climactic fireworks in the car

dump, a scene with Lester's wife and children in front of their house. Roy and others move out cots, etc., in case the house catches fire. Later, as Bubber is led away, there should be shots of the house burning, Lester's wife and children weeping.

12) There is a short scene missing at the end, and the order of the scenes on either side of it has been reversed. The last three sequences should run: *a* – Anna outside Val's house; she receives the news of Jake's death (the end of the film as it stands). *b* – Ruby packing things in the car. Edwin in his car – he has decided to leave. Emily drives up in *her* car, persuades him to stay; they drive home in their separate cars. *c* – Ruby and Calder leave (according to the script, Mrs Henderson is present again here – the only person to watch them go; there is no sign of her in the scene as it stands). This is clearly how the film should end: in fact, in my first few re-viewings of *The Chase* the ending with Anna and Val always took me by surprise – I had remembered the 'right' (and logical) ending. The last shot, with Anna walking slowly towards the camera as the credits come up, looks 'corny' as well as inappropriate.

Finally, it should be added that Penn disowns and detests the credit sequence, which he didn't shoot. I don't share his dislike; but certainly the credit sequence sets a tone which may partly account for the charge of 'hysteria' often levelled at the film (wrongly, in my opinion). Penn wanted plain credits.

It is evident that the aspect of the film that has suffered most in the cutting is the social background – especially the sense of omnipresent racial tensions. The moment near the beginning when the negro boy in the car sees the escaped convicts and is told by his mother not to meddle in 'white folks' business' would make far more sense could one see it as the first statement of a recurring motif: as it stands, it seems a slightly opportunistic irrelevance. None of the cut portions is strictly necessary to the film from a narrative viewpoint; none adds ideas or themes that aren't present elsewhere. There can be little doubt, however, that these scenes and details would add flesh to the film, giving aspects of it stronger emphasis and greater depth and fullness.

In view of all this, and of Penn's virtual disowning of the film, it would seem to be difficult rationally to defend my judgement of it as a masterpiece. Yet further viewings since I wrote on *The Chase* have given me no wish to retract. What is on the screen was all (the credit sequence apart) shot by Penn; if it is edited wrongly and the takes we see are sometimes 'second best', this only proves that, however important editing may be to Penn, it isn't the whole of his art, and that Penn's second best is better than most people's best. *The Chase* continues to look to me very much like a Penn film; and I must insist that Penn himself, far from offering an authoritive judgement, is probably the last person in the world to go to for an impartial view of what actually reached the screen: the intense frustrations and disillusionments he experienced on the film make his feelings about it not only understandable but inevitable. I am sure *The Chase* as it exists in Penn's mind is an even greater film than the one we have; but the spectator has the advantage over him of having no ideal *Chase* in his head against which to judge the current version, and can therefore view it without prejudice.

FILMOGRAPHY

Born Philadelphia, 1922. School in New York and New Hampshire, while living with his mother and his brother Irving Penn, the photographer. Went to live in Philadelphia with his father. Graduated from Olney High School where he had been involved in amateur dramatics and began to study watchmaking, his father's trade. 1943: enlisted US Army Infantry and went for training at Fort Jackson. Started a small theatre group where he met Fred Coe. Towards the end of the war joined Joshua Logan's theatre company. 1946: on demobilization went to Black Mountain College, North Carolina, then to the Universities of Perugia and Florence. Studied at Actors' Studio, and with Michael Chekhov in Los Angeles.

Television Work
1951: Floor manager at NBC on variety shows and news. Then floor manager on 'Colgate Comedy Hour'.

1953: wrote three TV plays, two for Ezio Pinza and one for Joan Caulfield and Mac-Donald Carey. Started directing 'First Per-son', an experimental show at NBC produced by Fred Coe and written by Paddy Chayefsky, Horton Foote, Robert Allan Aurthur, among others. Actors included Kim Stanley and Mildred Dunnock.

1953–55: directed 'Philco Playhouse', also produced by Fred Coe. There were thirteen shows per season and authors included Paddy Chayefsky, Horton Foote, Robert Allan Aurthur and David Shaw; among the actors were Kim Stanley, E. G. Marshall, Paul Newman, Joanne Woodward and Steve Hill.

1956: Directed 'The Miracle Worker' with Teresa Wright, Burl Ives and Patty McCormack, and Leslie Stevens' 'Portrait of a Murderer' for 'Playhouse 90'. Also directed 'Private Property' with Tab Hunter.

1958: directed 'Charley's Aunt' in 'Playhouse 90'.

1967: directed 'Flesh and Blood' with Kim Stanley, E. G. Marshall, Edmond O'Brien and Suzanne Pleshette for NBC.

139

Theatre Work	Films

Theatre Work

1954: directed 'Blue Denim'.

1957–58: directed Broadway production of 'Two for the Seesaw' by William Gibson with Anne Bancroft and Henry Fonda.

1958: wrote stage version of 'Fiorello'.

1959: directed 'The Miracle Worker' on Broadway with Anne Bancroft, Patty Duke and Patricia Neal.

1960: directed Broadway production of 'Toys in the Attic' by Lillian Hellman with Maureen Stapleton, Jason Robards and Irene Worth.

1960: directed 'An Evening with Nichols and May'.

1960: directed 'All the Way Home' by Tad Mosel on Broadway with Coleen Dewhurst and Arthur Hall.

1962: directed the Broadway production of 'In the Counting House' by Leslie Wiener with Sidney Chaplin and Howard da Silva.

1963: directed Broadway production of 'Lorenzo' by Jack Richardson with Alfred Drake and Fritz Weaver.

1964: directed Broadway musical 'Golden Boy' with Sammy Davis Jr.

1966: directed 'Wait until Dark' by Frederick Knott on Broadway with Lee Remick.

Films

1957 *The Left-Handed Gun*. Warner Bros. (A Harroll Production).
Directed by Arthur Penn. Produced by Fred Coe. Screenplay by Leslie Stevens from a play by Gore Vidal. Photographed by J. Peverell Marley. Art director: Art Loel. Sets by William L. Kuehl. Edited by Folmar Blangsted. Music by Alexander Courage; ballad by William Goyen and Alexander Courage. Assistant director: Russ Saunders. Sound: Earl Crain Sr. Costumes: Marjorie Best. Makeup: Gordon Bau. 102 minutes. British release version 87 minutes. U.S. release, May, 1958. With Paul Newman (William Bonney), Lita Milan (Celsa), John Dehner (Pat Garrett), Hurd Hatfield (Moultrie), James Congdon (Charlie Boudre), James Best (Tom Folliard), Colin Keith-Johnston (Tunstall), John Dierkes (McSween), Bob Anderson (Hill), Wally Brown (Moon), Ainslie Pryor (Joe Grant), Martin Garralaga (Saval), Denver Pyle (Ollinger), Paul Smith (Bell), Nestor Paiva (Maxwell), Jo Summers (Mrs Garrett), Robert Foulk (Brady), Anne Barton (Mrs Hill).

1962 *The Miracle Worker*. United Artists (A Playfilms Production).
Directed by Arthur Penn. Produced by Fred Coe. Screenplay by William Gibson from his own play 'The Miracle Worker'. Photographed by Ernest Caparros. Edited by Aram Avakian. Art direction: George Jenkins, Mel Bourne. Music by Laurence Rosenthal. Assistant directors: Larry Stuhran, Ulu Grossbord. Camera operator: Jack Horton.

140

Script supervisor: Maggie James. Costumes by Ruth Morley. 106 minutes. U.S. release July, 1962. With Anne Bancroft (Annie Sullivan), Patty Duke (Helen Keller), Victor Jory (Captain Keller), Inga Swenson (Kate Keller), Andrew Prine (James Keller), Kathleen Comegys (Aunt Ev), Beah Richards (Viney), Jack Hollander (Mr Anagnes), Michael Darden (Percy—ten years), Dale Ellen Bethea (Martha—ten years), Peggy Burke (Helen—seven years), Walter Wright Jr (Percy—eight years), Donna Bryan (Martha —seven years), Mindy Sherwood (Helen— five years), Diane Bryan (Martha—five years), Keith Moore (Percy—six years), Michele Farr (Young Annie—ten years), Allan Howard (Young Jimmie—eight years), Judith Lowry (1st crone), Wm F. Haddock (2nd crone), Helen Ludlum (3rd crone), Belle (dog). Oscars (1962): best actress (Anne Bancroft) and supporting actress (Patty Duke).

1963 *The Train*. Penn worked for a week filming some action scenes and exteriors; worked two days with Lancaster, then learned that Frankenheimer was to replace him at Lancaster's request.

1964 *Mickey One* Columbia (A Florin/Tatira Production).
Directed and produced by Arthur Penn. Screenplay by Alan Surgal. Photographed by Ghislain Cloquet. Edited by Aram Avakian; assistant editor: Marc Lamb. Production designer: George Jenkins. Art director: William Crawford. Music by Eddie Sauter; improvisations by Stan Getz; music direction by Jack Shaindlin. Assistant director: Russell Saunders. Associate producer: Harrison Starr.

Assistant to producer: Gene Lasko. Script supervisor: Roberta Hodes. Dialogue coach and casting director: Gene Lasko. Costumes: Domingo Rodriguez. 93 minutes. Premiere, Venice festival, 1965. U.S. release, October, 1965. With Warren Beatty (Mickey), Alexandra Stewart (Jenny), Hurd Hatfield (Castle), Franchot Tone (Ruby Lapp), Teddy Hart (Breson), Jeff Corey (Fryer), Kamatari Fujiwara (the Artist), Donna Michelle (the Girl), Ralph Foody (Police Captain), Norman Gottschalk (the Evangelist), Dick Lucas (Employment agent), Jack Goodman (Cafeteria manager), Jeri Jensen (Helen), Charlene Lee (the Singer), Benny Dunn (Nightclub comic), Denise Darnell (Stripper), Dick Baker (Boss at Shaley's), Helen Witkowski (Landlady), William Koza and David Crane (Art gallery patrons), Mike Fish (Italian restaurateur), Greg Louis and Gus Christy (Bartenders), David Eisen (Desk clerk), Robert Sickinger (Policeman), Lew Prentiss (Kismet boss), Grace Colette (B-girl), Boris Gregurevitch (Kismet comic), James Middleton (Iggie), Dink Freeman (Xanadu MC), Thomas Erhart, Darwin Apel, Mike Caldwell, Jack Reidy, Jan Jordan.

1965 *The Chase*. Columbia (Lone Star/ Horizon Production).
Directed by Arthur Penn. Produced by Sam Spiegel. Screenplay by Lillian Hellman, based on novel and play by Horton Foote, produced on stage by José Ferrer. Music by John Barry. Photographed by Joseph LaShelle and (uncredited) Robert Surtees in Technicolor and Panavision. Production Designer: Richard Day. Art director: Robert Luthart. Sets by Frank Tuttle. Edited by Gene Mil-

ford. Assistant Directors: Russell Saunders, Bob Templeton, C. M. 'Babe' Florence. Cameramen: Bill Norton, Bob Hosler and Genghe Noir. Production manager: Joe Wonder. Sound supervisor: Charles G. Rice. Sound: James Z. Flaster. Script supervisor: Marshall Schlom. Makeup by Ben Lane. Hair: Virginia Jones. Costumes by Donfeld. Special effects by Dave Koehler. Main Title by Maurice Binder. 122 minutes; in U.S.A., 135 minutes. U.S. Release, February, 1966. With Marlon Brando (Sheriff Calder), Jane Fonda (Anna Reeves), Robert Redford (Bubber Reeves), E. G. Marshall (Val Rogers), Angie Dickinson (Ruby Calder), Janice Rule (Emily Stewart), Miriam Hopkins (Mrs Reeves), Martha Hyer (Mary Fuller), Richard Bradford (Damon Fuller), Robert Duvall (Edwin Stewart), James Fox (Jake Jason Rogers), Diana Hyland (Elizabeth Rogers), Henry Hull (Briggs), Jocelyn Brando (Mrs Briggs), Katherine Walsh (Verna Dee), Lori Martin (Cutie), Marc Seaton (Paul), Paul Williams (Seymour), Clifton James (Lem), Malcolm Atterbury (Mr Reeves), Nudia Westman (Mrs Henderson), Joel Fluellen (Lester Johnson), Steve Ihnat (Archie), Maurice Manson (Moore), Bruce Cabot (Sol), Steve Whittaker (Slim), Pamela Curren (Mrs Sifftefieus), Ken Renard (Sam), Eduardo Ciannelli (Mr Sifftefieus), Grady Sutton and Richard Collier (guests at Rogers' party), Ralph Moody, George Winters, Howard Wright, Monte Hale, Mel Gallagher, Ray Galvin, Davis Roberts, Amy Fonda (young Anna in photo).

1967 *Bonnie and Clyde*. Warner Bros. (A Tatira-Hiller Production).

Directed by Arthur Penn. Produced by Warren Beatty. Screenplay by David Newman and Robert Benton. Photographed by Burnett Guffey in Technicolor. Art Director: Dean Tavoularis. Sets by Raymond Paul. Edited by Dede Allen. Music by Charles Strouse. Assistant director: Jack N. Reddish. Production manager: Russ Saunders. Assistant to producer: E. Michea. Script supervisor: John Dutton. Costumes: Theodora van Runkle, Andy Matyasi, Norma Brown. Special effects: Danny Lee. Special consultant: Robert Towne. Flatt and Scruggs 'Foggy Mountain Breakdown', courtesy Mercury records. 111 minutes. U.S. release July, 1967. With Warren Beatty (Clyde Barrow), Faye Dunaway (Bonnie Parker), Michael J. Pollard (C. W. Moss), Gene Hackman (Buck Barrow), Estelle Parsons (Blanche), Denver Pyle (Frank Hamer), Dub Taylor (Ivan Moss) Evans Evans (Velma Davis), Gene Wilder (Eugene Grizzard).

1969 *Alice's Restaurant* United Artists (A Florin Production).

Directed by Arthur Penn. Produced by Hillard Elkins and Joe Manduke. Screenplay by Venable Herndon and Arthur Penn, based on the recording 'The Alice's Restaurant Massacree' by Arlo Guthrie. Photographed in Technicolor by Michael Nebbia. Art Director: Warren Clymer. Set decorator: John Mortensen. Edited by Dede Allen. Original music by Arlo Guthrie. Musical supervision with additional music composed and arranged by Garry Sherman. 'Songs to Ageing Children' by Joni Mitchell; 'Pastures of Plenty' and 'Car Song' by Woody Guthrie. Musical director: Fred Hellerman. Associate producer: Harold

Leventhal. Production supervisor: Willard W. Goodman. Associate editor: Gerald Greenberg. Assistant editors: Richard Marks and Stephen Rotter. III minutes. U.S. release: August 1969. With Arlo Guthrie (Arlo), Pat Quinn (Alice), James Broderick (Ray), Michael McClanathan (Shelly), Geoff Outlaw (Roger), Tina Chen (Mari-Chan), Kathleen Dabney (Karin), Police Chief William Obanhein (Officer Obie), Seth Allen (evangelist), Monroe Arnold (Blueglass), Joseph Boley (Woody), Vinnette Carroll (lady clerk), Sylvia Davis (Marjorie), Simm Landres (Jacob), Eulalie Noble (Ruth), Louis Beachner (Dean), MacIntyre Dixon (first minister at deconsecration), Revd Dr Pierce Middleton (second minister), Donald Marye (funeral director), Shelly Plimpton (Rennie), M. Emmet Walsh (group W sergeant), Ronald Weyand (first policeman), Eleanor Wilson (landlady), Simon Deckard (doctor), Thomas De Wolfe (waiter), Judge James Hannon (himself), Graham Jarvis (music teacher), John Quill (second policeman), Frank Simpson (sergeant), Alice Brock, Pete Seeger, Lee Hays.

1970 *Little Big Man* Cinema Center (A Stockbridge-Hiller Production).
Directed by Arthur Penn. Produced by Stuart Millar. Screenplay by Calder Willingham from the novel by Thomas Berger. Photographed in Panavision and colour by Harry Stradling Sr. Art director: Dean Tavoularis. Edited by Dede Allen. With Dustin Hoffman (Little Big Man), Faye Dunaway (Mrs Pendrake), Richard Boone, Martin Balsam, Amy Eccles (Sunshine) Kelly Jean Peters (Olga), Cal Bellini (Younger Bear), etc.

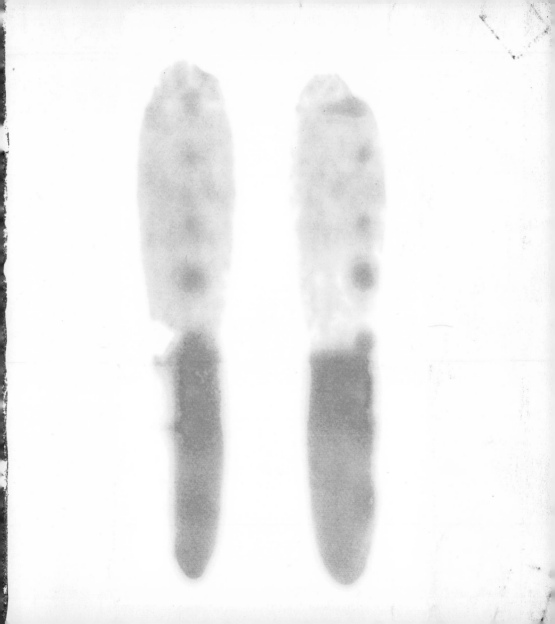

DATE DUE

MAY 1 2002		
IL6330487		
5/10/02		